**GROWING UP IN THE 40s**

**I·O·W·A
HERITAGE
COLLECTION**

GROWING UP
IN THE
40s

Rural Reminiscence

JERRY L. TWEDT

IOWA STATE UNIVERSITY PRESS / AMES

TO MY FAMILY
and all persons who share memories of
growing up in rural America during the 1940s

Jerry L. Twedt has a B.A. from Luther College, Decorah, Iowa, and a M.A. from the University of Illinois. He was a television producer-director for twenty-seven years. Twenty-three of those years were spent at Channel 7, WSVN, in Miami, Florida, where he twice won the N.A.T.P.E. Award for best locally produced performing arts program in the United States. He is currently a video producer for the Broward County Sheriff's Office in Fort Lauderdale, Florida. Mr. Twedt has published nine plays and several short stories and has written numerous television scripts.

Authorization to photocopy items for internal or personal use, or the internal or personal use of specific clients, is granted by Iowa State University Press, provided that the base fee of $.10 per copy is paid directly to the Copyright Clearance Center, 27 Congress Street, Salem, MA 01970. For those organizations that have been granted a photocopy license by CCC, a separate system of payments has been arranged. The fee code for users of the Transactional Reporting Service is 0-8138-2848-1/96 $.10.

♾ Printed on acid-free paper in the United States of America

First edition, 1994

Iowa Heritage Collection edition, 1996

International Standard Book Number: 0-8138-2848-1

Library of Congress Cataloging-in-Publication data is available

✐ CONTENTS

Introduction

I invite you to take a journey. For some, the journey will be familiar. It will be like plowing the back forty on a family owned farm or walking the streets one played upon as a child. For others, the journey will be quite strange, perhaps even surrealistic. These travelers may feel they have been transported, Star Trek style, to a different planet. Rest assured, however, that the journey will, indeed, be on earth, through a place known as central Iowa and a decade called the '40's. Understand, also, that your guide will be a child. Therefore, adult problems and momentous events will be largely ignored and simple pleasures, such as a Saturday night in town, will have monumental importance. But before we begin our journey, you should have some knowledge of the area you are about to visit.

On a warm June day in 1865, a train of eighteen covered wagons halted in what is now Howard Township, Story County, Iowa. The sweating horses and oxen welcomed the rest. They did not realize that their journey was over. The human members of the train, however, were well aware that the objective of nearly a month's travel from Lisbon, Illinois had been reached. The twelve families and two single men climbed down

The Harris Twedt Family, 1947

Standing:	*Herma, age 14; Jerry, age 12*
Sitting:	*Paul, age 7; Pete, age 17; Myrtle; Harris*
Kneeling:	*Linda, age 3*

from their nineteenth century mobile homes, congratulated themselves, and surveyed the land they had purchased for one dollar and twenty-five cents an acre.

The gently rolling prairie that greeted their blue Norwegian eyes held little resemblance to the manicured farm land of today. The lush grasses stood waist high to a grown man and nearly covered huge boulders which had been deposited during the last ice age. The settlers also were to discover large sloughs and treacherous quicksand. Many of these weary pioneers, who set about preparing their evening meal, must have wondered if this land in which they had invested everything was worth the hard cash paid.

In the decade that followed the coming of the original party, other Norwegians duplicated their trek, and the northern part of Story County was quickly populated. Acre by acre, land was cleared and the swamps drained. "Sod Buster" plows pulled by straining horses or oxen became a common sight. Virgin prairie was turned to the sun and planted in flax, oats, wheat, and corn. By 1870, there was little open prairie left in Howard Township and ten years later, the work of turning a wilderness into productive farms was complete.

As the farms of the area increased in number and productivity, the need for a town to service the farmers' and their families' needs, became apparent. In 1870, a post office was established and in 1873, a general store was opened. The town received a big boost when the railroad arrived in 1881. One year later, this thriving village consisted of two general stores, a hardware store, one furniture store, a dressmaking and millinery shop, one grocery, a restaurant, a hard and sweet cider establishment, three blacksmith shops, two shoemaker shops, a harness shop, one grain buyer and coal dealer, a lumber yard, a creamery, and two farm implement stores. This thriving village was named Roland.

Fifty-three years later, July 3, 1935, to be exact, a great grandson of one of the pioneer families was born. Me. And like those early pioneers, I flourished beneath the warm Iowa sun. What follows are recollections of my early years. Years which seem like yesterday, but were almost a life time ago.

Roland Consolidated School

ळ्क्ष **Roland Consolidated School**

It is not supposed to happen. A school is forever. A school is frozen in time, the keeper of your childhood. It is a never changing factor in an ever changing world. It gives you a happy feeling of permanence, of belonging, just to pass by your school. It remembers you. The school witnessed your successes and your failures. It shared your joys and your sorrows. There is no pretending with your school. It knows you, really knows you. You may drive up to it in an expensive car made in Germany, or approach its doors dressed in designer clothes direct from Paris, but the school is unimpressed. Your essence is imbedded in the brick and mortar.

But it does happen. Nothing is forever, not even a school. My school, Roland Consolidated School, Roland, Iowa, was torn down in 1988. In its place, stands a modern facility. From the graduates, who wandered far from the town and school, comes the plaintive question, "Why? Couldn't the old building be saved?" The equally plaintive answer came from those who stayed, "No. The old place was falling apart. Nothing could be done."

Nothing, that is, but remember. And that we did on July

8

2nd, 1988, when an all school reunion was held. Those of us who measured our progress by what classroom we entered in September, once again, walked the halls and recalled when running was our normal gait, and dreams were not only possible, but certain.

The basic facts concerning the school can be told quickly. On a cold January day in 1914, the people of the Roland community voted to consolidate four rural school districts with the Roland Independent School. An architect was hired. In the spring, contracts were let in the amount of fifty-two thousand dollars for a two story building with a basement. The corner stone for the one hundred and four feet long by seventy-eight feet wide building was laid December 7, 1915. Dedication services were held September 29, 1916. The building could never be mistaken for anything but a school. Its red brick construction and rectangular design were almost identical to every other school in the mid-west.

The interior was as similar to surrounding schools as the exterior. The basement contained home economics, the music room, and the gymnasium. (Once the new gym was built in 1941, the old one became a lunch room.) Dominating the first floor was a great hall, around which were large windowed rooms. The first six grades, plus a teachers' lounge, the superintendent's office, the religion room, the boys' bathroom, and the mysterious girls' bathroom into which all boys were forbidden to peek, were on this floor. The second floor was almost a carbon copy of the first, including an even more mysterious girls' bathroom into which all boys were peeking.

9

Instead of a large hall, there was an assembly room. This room had a small stage, which was usually graced with an out-house every Halloween, and desks for each high school student.

Along with the high school, the seventh and eighth grades also were located on the second floor. It was a real benchmark in a child's life when he entered seventh grade. He was then on the same floor as the big kids!

The average class size during the '40s and '50s was between fifteen and twenty-five. My sister Herma's class (1951) was the smallest. It had only twelve. The total number in high school averaged eighty-five. Due to the small size, everyone knew everyone else. In fact, most of us were related.

It was to this school that I, timidly, ventured in the fall of 1941. And it was from this same solid, unpretentious edifice that I emerged, diploma in hand, twelve years later.

For a farm child, the school day began with arrival of the bus. This could be as early as seven-twenty if you were one of the first to be picked up. The sighting of the bus triggered a mad scramble for coats, followed by a dash down the lane. Once aboard, there was nothing to do but settle down for a long ride. While most of these rides were boring, they did prove to be an education in themselves. Every so often, I would finish assignments or study for tests, but mostly I dedicated my time to learning more important things: Hearts and Blackjack; the proper way to aim a bean shooter; how to shoot paper wads; the art of smuggling a loaded water pistol past the bus driver; matching pennies; and, when to stop whatever I was doing to avoid being thrown off of the bus!

Two very important "firsts" happened to me aboard the bus. I gazed upon my first cleavage, and I delivered my first and only bloody nose.

The cleavage belonged to a sweet young thing of about thirteen. I was sitting across the aisle from her, and we were talking about somebody. That somebody must have been on the bus, because I leaned across the aisle to whisper something into her ear. She bent toward me. Voila! There they were! Unbraed! Not too large, I'll admit, but very much the real thing. Needless to say, I spent the rest of the bus ride thinking up all sorts of secrets that my lips confided in her ear while my eyes roamed the blossoming mounds. I am quite sure she knew exactly what I was doing. Subtle I was not. And, since she knew, she must have enjoyed the episode as much as I. I wonder if she remembers? Some day, when she has her grandchildren gathered around, I'll ask.

I've seen a lot of nose bleeds. Had my share. But I've never seen anything like the gusher I created when I was seven. It all began when Charlene Hall, a classmate and neighbor, began teasing me. She kept passing notes saying, "Jerry loves so and so." Each note contained the name of a different girl in our class. At the time, I considered Charlene to be a royal pain in the neck. She would come over to play with my sister, Herma, but somehow always seemed to foul up my day by getting me involved.

The bus was almost to our farm when Charlene wrote the name of the girl I did like. In the parlance of today, I lost it. My right fist landed a direct hit on Charlene's pretty nose. The tears and blood began flowing simultaneously. Everyone on the bus attempted to help Charlene. Even I offered her an almost clean handkerchief. My anger quickly turned to fear. I had never hit anyone in the face before, and the blood pouring from Charlene's nose frightened me almost as much as it did her.

Herma could not wait to tell Mother, who in turn gave the bloody details to Dad. His reaction was swift and aimed toward the rear portion of my anatomy. I was not the only one who landed a direct hit that day.

The following afternoon, when we were ready to be dismissed from school, Miss Cunningham told me to report to the superintendent's office. The class sat in stunned silence as I walked from the room. Nobody else in the second grade had committed a sin so grievous as to warrant the attention of the superintendent.

Mr. Gorton was the superintendent's name. As I fearfully approached his desk, he was reading a newspaper. I stood there for what seemed to be forever before he glanced over his paper.

"So, you're the one who hit the little girl," he said, again putting the newspaper between us.

"Yes...yes, sir," I answered in a small voice.

He paused for a moment, then said, "That wasn't very nice, was it."

I shook my head.

Not hearing a response, Mr. Gorton again looked over his paper. "Well, was it?"

"No! It...it was bad." I felt the first two tears crawl down my face.

"You won't do it again, will you?" Mr. Gorton asked, as he returned to his newspaper.

The first two tears crawled. Those that followed ran. "No...no, sir," I sniffled.

"Good," Mr. Gorton replied.

A long silence followed. I could not believe I was not to be spanked, so I remained standing in front of the desk, waiting for Mr. Gorton to get his huge paddle that I had been told he kept in a closet. He did not move. Finally, from behind the newspaper, came the words, "You can go."

I went!

I have often thought about this episode, and am now convinced that he hid behind that blasted newspaper so I would not see that he was laughing!

As for Charlene, she didn't tease me much after that. The fact is, she pretty much lost all interest in me. This made me happy. However, like the song says, "Little girls get bigger every day." Charlene grew into a beautiful, statuesque blond, who had most of the boys drooling. The situation between us was then reversed. I tried to get her attention, and she considered me a royal pain in the neck!

There was another memorable bus ride. The first. I can remember (yes, like it was yesterday) holding Herma's hand as the bus pulled to a stop at the end of our lane. I had looked forward to this day for months. But now that it was here, I was one frightened six-year-old. Had Herma not been holding my hand, I think I would have run back to Mother. The bus seemed huge! And as I climbed the steps, I felt very small. I sat close beside Herma all the way to school and did not say a word. I am sure it is the only time in my life that I was on a school bus and said nothing.

Herma delivered me to the first grade room and left me in the capable hands of a pretty young teacher named Miss Burger. I still do not know her first name. I think that is because elementary school teachers do not have first names. They are always Miss, Mrs., or Mr. something or other. Perhaps their first names are taken away when they sign contracts!

There were about twenty-five frightened children in the room, children who for the first time had no mothers nearby to wipe away the tears. Miss Burger began by introducing each and everyone of us. This was actually unnecessary, as most of us had first met when members of the yowling choir in the church nursery.

In fact, Miss Burger spent the entire year making introductions. She introduced us to the glorious art of finger painting (loved it), to staying within the lines when coloring (failed miserably), to the mysteries of telling time, the alphabet, and numbers (struggled, but made progress), and to reading. From the beginning, reading was magic. I learned all about Dick and Jane and their dog Tags. I read about how they walked, ran, sat, slept, jumped, laughed, cried, and...well, you know. You probably read the same book! Remember how, whatever it was, Dick would do it first, then Jane, then Tags? Dick ran down the hill. Jane ran down the hill. Tags ran down the hill. Not much of a plot, but the pictures were great. However, the story I remember best was not about Dick and Jane and was at the end of the book. It concerned a sad, lonely house that sat on a hill. The house was sad because no one lived in it. Along came this little boy and girl who were also sad and lonely, because they had no place to live. The children decided to live in the house, and they and the house were happy. I felt very sorry for the house, but fear and dread for the children. Having no parents to care for you and no place to live is powerful stuff when you're six.

I loved first grade. Miss Burger made learning fun and soon molded us into a class which cared for each other. This we maintained throughout our elementary and high school years. We became an extended family. Oh, we had our fights, just ask Charlene. But, if one of the older kids picked on a class member, he or she felt the wrath of the whole group. I suppose this "togetherness" is one of the major differences between attending a small, consolidated school and a large, urban one. In a large school, there are too many children for just one class per age group. You, therefore, never have the same people in a class year after year. At Roland Consolidated, we did. Of the twenty-five who attended Miss Burger's first grade, sixteen of us shared every step of our twelve year journey.

The most fun part of the journey was recess! Nothing unusual about that. Every kid loves recess. But, unless you were raised on a farm, you will never know what a joy it was to have a whole room full of children to play with. And play we did!

For the younger set there were swings, a merry-go-round, trick poles, and lots of room to play "Red Rover, Red Rover." A heavily shrubbed portion in the northeast corner of the playground was great for "hide and seek" and "cowboys and Indians". The older kids had areas for baseball and football, plus the tennis court on which to play basketball. If they grew tired of team sports, there was plenty of room to dig a hole and play "Pot". Not smoke it! Play it!

"Pot" was a marble game. A small hole was dug. Each player put in a marble. Then, a line was drawn about ten feet behind the hole, and each boy (we never allowed girls to play) took his turn at attempting to toss his "shooter", a large marble called a boulder, into the hole. The player who achieved this won the pot. If nobody won, then more marbles were added for the next round. A good pot could contain twenty marbles. Anyone who could consistently win these large pots was considered a high roller. I was not. My draw string marble sack was usually much lighter leaving school than upon arrival.

During the winter, the center of activity was the ice skating pond. The pond was created by opening the fire hydrant on the east side of the playground, just south of the tennis courts. This always was done on a Friday, so that the water would have the weekend to freeze solid. The following Monday was one to which every child in school looked forward. Small bodies flew every which direction, and more than a few tears were shed by the kids on skates for the first time. There was no trouble spotting them. They were the ones who stood hunched over a few feet from the edge, ankles collapsed, not daring to move either leg. They were ignored by hot shots who could skate backwards and were able to come to precise ice scraping halts. Most of us fell some place in between and enjoyed games of tag, racing, or playing "crack the whip".

My first skates were a rusty pair of clamp-ons. Even after being cleaned and sharpened, they were nearly impossible to use. The tightening mechanisms on the toe clamps were worn, and no matter how hard I tried to secure the skates, they continually fell off. I would no more than get started when one of the clamps would release and send me face down on the ice.

By Christmas of 1944, I was fed up. I let it be known to anyone in my family who would listen that I wanted a pair of shoe skates. This request was a problem for my parents. Due to World War II, there were no shoe skates being made. My dad even tried to buy used skates. There were none to be had.

On Christmas morning, I ran downstairs and was rewarded with the sight of shoe skates! However, my joy turned to disappointment when I discovered they were the same skates my older brother, Pete, had outgrown. I wore size four. The skates were size eight! Mother and Dad explained the situation, and I decided that an over-sized pair of skates was better than none at all. I compensated for the largeness by stuffing cotton into the toes. I also wore several pair of heavy wool socks. For the next four years, I could tell how much my feet had grown by seeing how much cotton I had to remove from each skate.

How well a person skated was insignificant. The important thing was the ritual that accompanied skating and the companionship provided. First, was the anticipation we all felt as the clock neared recess time. When the bell rang, we charged from our seats, grabbed our skates, and dashed for the back stairwell. There, with much laughing and talking, we lined our shoes on the steps and raced to see who could get his skates on first. Then, walking on the points of our skates, it was out into the wintry air for fifteen minutes of nonstop action. What you did was unimportant. That you did it at top speed and in full voice was.

When our fun was interrupted by our teacher, we slowly trooped back into the building, and, taking as much time as possible, removed our skates and reclaimed our shoes. Returning to the classroom, we put our wet mittens on the radiators and went back to work. The radiators sizzled while a miniature ground fog arose from the soggy hand gear. Within minutes, the air was permeated with the smell of drying wool. I can still smell it. All I have to do is watch ice skating on television, and traces of that pungent odor filter into my mind on vapor trails of childhood memories.

Our room teacher taught everything except music and religion. For those classes, we journeyed to the music room and the religion room. Having a room devoted to religion was accepted as normal. Most of us were surprised when we discovered other schools did not have daily classes in religion as part of the standard curriculum. In religion class, we learned the ten commandments, memorized the books of the Bible, sang songs, read Bible stories, and suffered through Luther's Catechism. This was all possible because of the homogeneous make-up of the school district. Only two families in the community were not of Norwegian ancestry and the Lutheran faith.

Our religion teachers, on the whole, were well trained and good instructors. I especially remember Miss Holthe. She was a warm, loving woman, whom we all respected and loved. But there were two, who, although dedicated and well meaning, could not relate well to children. Both were over emotional, cried easily, and were unable to handle naughty little boys.

Two stories come to mind.

Miss X, as I shall call her, was lecturing on the proper way to treat the Bible. As usual, a small group of boys in the back row were causing trouble. Miss X attempted to ignore them and spoke at great length to the rest of the class about the Bible being the holy word of God and that it must always be handled reverently. The group of boys became more and more unruly. Finally, Miss X angrily ordered them to be quiet. The silence must have lasted for at least four seconds, then one boy began to laugh. His behavior so infuriated Miss X that she literally ran around behind the last row of chairs and hit the offending boy over the head with the Bible!

Miss Y was having similar problems. It was always the boys who caused all the trouble. The girls did nothing but pass notes and enjoy the torment caused by the boys! Well, toward the close of an especially trying session, Miss Y decided she was going to call on a higher authority. She dismissed the rest of the class and kept the five offending boys in the room. The boys were ordered to their knees. Miss Y then began to pray for them. She reminded them that God was watching every move they made and that they should mend their ways. She prayed they would be good boys, and that they would grow into God-fearing men. The boys responded by giggling. This was too much for Miss Y. She was reduced to tears. So, there they were - five thirteen-year-old boys practically rolling on the floor with laughter as a middle-aged women wept and prayed for their immortal souls. I think heaven received some very mixed signals that day. Miss Y's lips asked God to guide and lead these boys to the true path. But I have the feeling her heart was asking for something quite different. Come to think of it, that room did get rather warm!

Miss X and Miss Y were not representative of Roland's teachers. On the whole, they were excellent. Some were superior. I had only one bad teacher. He was a nice man who attempted to teach physics to an all boy class. The poor man lasted one semester. I am sure we drove him out of the pro-fession...or at least up to the college ranks. In his class, I learned but one law of physics. It is as follows: The decibel level of the cry is directly proportional to the velocity of and the distance traveled by the chalk board eraser!

Most of my elementary teachers were just out of college. They were young and pretty, and I was a little bit in love with each of them. I remember a twinge of jealousy when my fifth grade teacher, Mazel Hoversten, became engaged to Bob Birkeland. (If an elementary school teacher is a local girl and comes back to teach, she is allowed to have a first name.) But there was one teacher who was not young, not pretty, and who I did not love at all. Mrs. Christopherson!

Mrs. Christopherson was old. She was so old she had taught my uncle, who was then a soldier. Her hair was gray, her face was broad, and her body...well, to be kind, I will call it matronly. A large nose, which could smell trouble while a kid was still on the school bus, dominated her squarish face. On that nose rested rimless glasses, which enlarged steel blue eyes that could strike fear even into the hearts of other teachers!

Mrs. Christopherson taught fourth grade. No, that is not quite true. She ruled fourth grade. She was an absolute dictator. There was no court of appeals. Her students did what they were told, when they were told, or else! And as a child, you had no desire to find out about the "or else". It is, therefore, not surprising that the third grade class spent the last half of the year wandering the halls whispering prayers of the condemned. Each member spent his or her time in the religion room fervently asking God that Mrs. Christopherson be taken to her heavenly reward. Or, at least, that she move to Ames! I personally thought being trampled by a stampeding herd of Texas Longhorns would be an appropriate end.

God saw fit not to answer our prayers.

On a gloomy day, in the fall of 1944, my classmates and I began serving our fourth grade sentence. Some of us were pale. Some near tears. Our time of trial was at hand. Mrs. Christopherson greeted us at the door with a smile. But this did not fool anyone! We knew that once the door was shut, she would turn into a three-headed monster whose favorite food was nine-year-old boy roasted slowly over a spit! There was no escape. The only hope we shared was that those who had gone before us had survived. Never, in the history of the world, has any class been so quiet or so fearful. Had Mrs. Christopherson so much as said, "boo", she would have had puddles under twenty-five chairs.

She did not, of course. She simply took us in hand and began teaching us everything she could cram into our little Norwegian heads. There were no discipline problems. If we even thought about misbehaving boys, all she had to do was look at us, and the room became as quiet as a church when the preacher forgets his sermon.

Under the tutelage of this dower woman, I learned division, increased my reading comprehension by three grades, and acquired a love of history that continues to this day. However, she was not omnipotent. Even Mrs. Christopherson failed to teach me how to spell.

Did we pass unto the class behind us that Mrs. Christopherson would be the best teacher they would ever have? Don't be silly. We told them what we had been told. We rolled our eyes and whispered as if she could hear us, "Wait until next year! She'll eat you alive!"

For any child to learn, there first must be an atmosphere conducive to learning. Such an atmosphere existed at Roland Consolidated, largely through the efforts of the school superintendent, Mr. C.P. Thompson, and the high school principal,

Mrs. Cecil Finch. Perhaps part of their success was due to their close interaction with the students. Mrs. Finch taught math and was director of vocal music for all twelve grades. Mr. Thompson taught typing and was director of the junior and high school bands. The two lost no respect through this familiarity and gained a great deal of affection.

Mr. Thompson came to Roland during my third year; however, I did not get to know him until the fifth grade, when I began playing coronet in the junior band. He was of above average height and had a football player build through the chest and shoulders. His face was round, his eyes were gentle, and he parted his thinning gray hair in the middle. Although Mr. Thompson could be tough, he was a highly sentimental man. He often wept at graduation ceremonies.

He also was a patient man. Not by nature, but because of powerful self control. Much of this control was developed directing the junior band each Wednesday morning at eleven fifteen.

Attending junior band practice was somewhat like going "through the looking glass". I remember one day when Larry Boten, a fellow cornet player, was producing the weirdest sound ever to come out of a horn. It was so strange that Mr. Thompson stepped down from the podium and crossed to Larry's chair. He asked Larry to play the scale. Larry tried, but each note sounded like it had been forced through a strainer.

Mr. Thompson glared at Larry. "Have you been practicing?"

"Yeah!" Larry said defensively. "I practiced last night."

Perhaps unwilling to believe the sound he had heard, Mr. Thompson asked Larry to play the scale again. Larry did and Mr. Thompson believed.

"That's awful! Is something wrong with your horn?"

Poor Larry was so frightened he did not know what to say. He knew that Mr. Thompson would not stand for an instrument being blamed for sloppy playing or lack of practice. "It...it does blow sorta' hard," he gulped.

Mr. Thompson snatched the horn from Larry's hand, pulled out the mouth piece, and turned the cornet upside down. Out fell a long tinker toy stick!

"I...I didn't put there!" Larry cried. "Honest! It must have been my little brother."

Mr. Thompson handed the horn back to Larry, shook his head, and returned to the relative sanity of the podium.

When I was in sixth grade, Mr. Thompson asked me if I would switch from the cornet to the baritone. As the school owned the instrument and the mouth piece was twice the size of a cornet's, I agreed. Little did I realize that the school's fine baritone player, Jimmy Hansen, was graduating, and that I would be expected to take his place the following year. (If good enough, a student could join the high school band while in junior high.) Thus, it came to pass, in the seventh year of my sojourn through Roland Consolidated, I became the first chair baritone player in a one baritone band. The prestige I enjoyed. The responsibility was something else. Whenever a selection called for a baritone solo, everyone held their breath. The problem was that I sometimes joined them. Do you know how quiet it is in an auditorium when the conductor is beating time and nobody is playing? I do.

Due to fine teaching by Mr. Thompson and hard work on the part of the band members, Roland had an excellent concert band. Each of my six years in the band ended with a superior rating in the state music contest. Because of this rating, we were invited to play at the Iowa State Fair. We gave one performance during the morning and another in the late afternoon. The rest of the day was ours to do as we wished. And what we wished was the MIDWAY!

The midway was everything Roland was not: exciting, tempting, crowded, noisy, smelly, and filled with things we shouldn't eat, shouldn't touch, and shouldn't see! Naturally, we loved it. My friends and I would first zero in on the best ride ever created...the bumper cars! We would ride the bumper cars three or four times in a row before even looking at anything else. Hitting a car in the rear going full out was one of the true delights of my childhood. It was even more special if the car were driven by a classmate or friend. The anticipation of the ride as I strapped myself in and waited for the electricity to flow, was tremendous. I would plot my strategy, seeing where I had to drive so as to avoid a huge pile up. There are few things more frustrating than sitting in a tangle of bumper cars unable to move. And there are few things more exhilarating than to avoid a pile up, circle the entire rink at full speed, and bang into your chosen target. There is no doubt that my Viking blood boiled over when I was behind the wheel of a bumper car.

As much as we loved our bumper cars, there were other things on the midway that aroused the blood of growing boys. When my friends and I turned sixteen, we decided to enter one of these dens of iniquity. The most daring part of this episode was standing in line to get in. We had two worries: one, that our parents might see us; two, that the barker would ask for an ID and not let us in. Our fears were groundless on both counts.

We entered the long, narrow tent and walked toward the simple portable stage. Unlike church, we sat as close to the front as possible. We did our best to appear cool and worldly, but fooled no one. Our beardless faces were flushed with erotic mental images, and nervous giggles punctuated our conversation. None of us had ever felt so deliciously sinful!

Show time came and the rather unruly crowd, made up mostly of young bucks and dirty old men, began to applaud and chant, "Bring on the girls!" After a few moments of this, the lights went out, the stage lights were turned on, and the dancing began. I don't know about the other guys, but my pulse rate must have been a least one hundred and fifty!

Alas, our images were much better than the show. The girls could not dance, and they did not strip. All they did was jump around. Having an older sister, I had seen more at home than I saw during the first part of that so called "strip tease". My heart beat quickly returned to normal.

I can honestly say, that, until the final act, I was bored. Then the star came out, and we were treated to the real thing! Accompanied by drums and cries of "Take it off!", she provocatively wiggled her way down to a "G" string and two pasties with tassels. For her finale, she began to rotate her large breasts. The tassels made sweeping arcs that made our young eyes bulge! A trumpet wailed, the drums beat an ever increasing tempo, and colored spotlights slashed across her writhing body. The tassels became spinning blurs! We were all on our feet screaming! Still faster rotated her breasts! My friends and I had never imagined a woman could do something like this! Her talent had never been covered in biology class at dear, old Roland High. And it certainly had not been discussed in the religion room. (Miss Holthe would not have approved!) When it seemed the tassels were about to propel her mammillary glands into an earth orbit, she pulled off the pasties and the lights went out!

Exiting the tent, we all agreed the last act had been something to see. But we debated whether the show as a whole had been worth the price of three rides on our beloved bumper cars!

Roland Consolidated also had excellent vocal music. In the annual music contest, the school entered a sixty voice choir and boys' and girls' glee clubs numbering thirty plus each. As I have already mentioned, the vocal music was under the direction of Mrs. Finch.

Mrs. Finch was, and is, a woman of wit and charm. When I was in school, she was fortyish, yet retained a youthful bounce and outlook. She was a fascinating person. Her eyes could shoot fire when angry and sparkle with devilish glee when happy. She loved kids, had a brilliant mind, and was blessed with a great sense of humor. She had the ability to make a student believe he could sing even if his voice was more suited to hog calling. She was a confident woman and was able to transfuse her confidence into the student. We all loved her.

I never think of Mrs. Finch without remembering my first music contest. I was singing in the mixed chorus because of a weak tenor section. To bolster the tenors, Mrs. Finch recruited three boys from the eighth grade. We actually could have sung soprano as our voices had not yet changed.

The contest fell on a dreary, miserable day. All music directors dread such days because bad weather usually causes poor performances. To make matters worse, we were one of the last choirs to sing. It was well after dark when we put on our maroon robes and white collars and climbed onto the bus. The bus was required because the building in which we were singing was some distance from the main contest area. It also was drizzling. Poor Mrs. Finch! Sixty grumpy tired teenagers crammed into one stuffy uncomfortable bus. It had to be her worst nightmare come true. As we approached our destination, the drizzle became a torrent. Sheets of rain enveloped the bus, obliterating the nearby buildings and street lights. We all groaned. We were trapped. Windows quickly fogged over. Sixty young bodies began to sweat. Robes that had been carefully pressed took on the appearance of a sale rack at a crowded flea market. Any chance we had of a superior rating was being washed down the storm drains with the rushing water.

It was then that Mrs. Finch ordered us to sing. We looked at each other in near shock. Nobody felt like singing. But when Mrs. Finch said sing, we sang.

Our contest selection was "Going Home". The music is from Dvorak's New World Symphony and has as its base the negro spiritual. It is a hauntingly beautiful work.

After only a few measures, we all knew something very special was happening. Perhaps it was because our bleak mood fit the sad dejection of the song. Whatever the reason, the music we made flowed with meaning and depth. We were singing with one voice. There was this strange sensation that nothing else existed. Nothing else mattered. Only the song. We poured our young souls into the music. I think we were as close to the angels as most of us will ever get.

The rain ceased as the last notes drifted into the low spent clouds. No one spoke. No one wanted to break the spell. Several of the girls were crying.

The ancient Greeks called it catharsis...a purging of emotions through art. Certainly, this is what we experienced. As we left the bus and marched onto the stage to sing, all of the day's petty irritations had been replaced by a feeling of serenity. We knew we had a superior rating won before we opened our mouths.

When we finished, there was a hush in the hall. We had sung well. But the performance was pale when compared to those moments of pure beauty that we shared in the bus.

Roland created music of another sort on the basketball floor. This music brought state wide recognition. The school fielded a girls' and boys' team, and, although the girls were good, it was the boys who excelled. With approximately forty boys in high school, the Roland Rockets established a record that was the envy of every school in the state. From 1948 through 1960, the team won 381 games and lost thirty, for a winning percentage of .927. The best year was 1951: thirty-five victories and one defeat; the worst: 1956, twenty-two wins and five losses. Out of these years came six All-State players and one collegiate All-American.

The objective of every high school team was to compete in the state basketball tournament in Iowa City. Until 1956, this tournament was called the "Sweet Sixteen". The top sixteen teams, regardless of enrollment, competed. Schools with less than one hundred played those who had over one thousand. Under this system, the Rockets won fourth place twice and were second once. The year we were second, 1951, was a classic David and Goliath confrontation that is still remembered by many. For those of us who were students, it is a memory that will never die, not even dim.

The 1951 season began with no thought of going to the state tournament. This was to be a rebuilding year. The eager group, who responded to Coach Buck Cheadle's call for tryouts, was not one to warm a coach's heart. There was little experience and less height. The team averaged less than five-foot-nine. The front court was made up of three seniors: six-foot-one Ralph Johnson and five-foot-eleven Frank Egland at forward, and five-foot-eleven Jake Hill at center. The back court consisted of Don Holland, a five-foot-seven junior, and a five-foot-six sophomore named Gary Thompson. Not much to brag about.

There were assets, however, the greatest being Coach Cheadle. Every boy out for basketball worshipped him. He was from Oklahoma and his high cheek bones, raven hair, and dark complexion were constant reminders of his Cherokee blood. Cheadle smiled easily, but there was an underlying explosiveness about him that was a little frightening. He demanded and received complete dedication. Not only did the boys out for basketball not drink or smoke, we didn't even eat candy bars! Coach Cheadle was a winner and was not about to let us be anything else. Had he put on eagle feathers and called us to do battle, we would have followed.

I was out for the team, and even though I never so much as suited up, I worked my tail off. I was not alone. Everyone was dragging by the end of practice. We were in constant motion... working the fast break, set plays, and defense, especially defense. Coach Cheadle believed no team could be a champion without superior defense. He loved to say, "On offense you're glory boys, but on defense, you're just scrawny kids in shorts and jerseys." Defense was stressed to the point that players bragged as much about the shots they blocked as the ones they made. Much to everyone's surprise, this drilling paid off with a thirty-two and zero record and a chance to play in the state tournament.

Our first game was with Hull, a small school located near Sioux City. The game was played in the afternoon, and there is no doubt that you could have dropped a bomb on Roland and not have hurt a soul. The whole town, farmers included, were in the University of Iowa field house watching the Rockets play. The game turned out to be somewhat of a bore. We won by nearly twenty points, 65-46. As usual, our defense was excellent, and we scored well on offense. Gary Thompson and Don Holland both had hot hands and were hitting from eighteen and twenty feet out.

Naturally, we were delighted with the victory. The press and radio commentators could not have cared less. What ink we did receive was rather patronizing. It was obvious that no one took us seriously. After all, one small school beating another was unimportant. The real story was the three way battle expected between Davenport, the perennial champion, East Des Moines, the tallest team in the tournament, and West Waterloo, considered to be the best team in the state. Roland was not in the picture.

Two days later, we faced West Waterloo. Nobody, not even the most loyal of us, expected a Roland victory. Certainly, the team from West Waterloo did not. During the pre-game warm-ups, it radiated confidence. It never occurred to the West Waterloo players that they might lose. Neither did the radio sportscasters consider the possibility. They were busily thinking of ways to make the expected blowout sound interesting. When the teams gathered for the opening tip off, no one in the field house realized that an Iowa basketball legend was about to be born.

West Waterloo gained an early lead, but was unable to make it a substantial one. Each time West Waterloo seemed on the verge of breaking the game wide open, Roland would close the gap. The West Waterloo players found this extremely frustrating. Even more frustrating for them was the tempo of the game. Roland played a slow, half court, high percentage shot type of game. We had no choice. Due to our lack of height, we had to hit a high percentage.

However, the most unsettling thing of all for the West Waterloo team was a five-foot-six-inch guard with floppy socks. Gary Thompson was driving them crazy. The West Waterloo five were playing a basic zone defense, which forced us to shoot from outside. This was Gary's game. With the calm precision of an accountant, Gary scored basket after basket from what is now three point range.

The field house began to come to life. People were slowly becoming aware that the game was not going to be a blowout, and the natural instinct to root for the underdog began to take hold. Thousands who had never heard of Roland found themselves yelling like local fans. The possibility of an upset was in the air and everyone knew it!

At half time, West Waterloo still led, but by a small margin. It was a far less confident team that left the floor than had arrived earlier. The spectators gathered in small groups to marvel at Gary's shooting and debate whether or not Roland could maintain the pace in the second half. Most shook their heads. The size and depth of the West Waterloo team would tell in the end. This was conventional basketball wisdom, but the Rockets were not a conventional team.

The second half began with Gary hitting one of his long, one-handed, push shots, and the crowd went crazy. He served notice that the first half had not been a fluke. The fans fell in love with him. Every time he shot, the field house became eerily quiet, then, if he made the basket, the place would erupt.

Waterloo's defensive strategy in the second half was focused on stopping Gary. However, by bringing a man out to keep Gary from shooting the long one, the middle was opened up, and his four team mates began hitting ten and fifteen foot shots. Like water eroding soil, Roland decreased West Waterloo's lead. The narrowing margin caused the fans to become more and more excited, and the West Waterloo boys to hurry their shots.

In the fourth quarter, Roland evened the score, then went ahead. The roar from the crowd was unbelievable! With less than four minutes to play and enjoying a small lead, Roland went into a freeze. As any basketball fan knows, a freeze can save you or kill you. The outcome all depends on ball handling.

During the last tension racked minutes, the only calm people in the field house were the Roland players. With all the emotion of farmers cultivating corn, they put on a dazzling display of dribbling and passing. The frantic efforts of the West Waterloo team failed. The final buzzer sounded and some staid Norwegians, along with other fans, went slightly crazy. Roland had pulled the upset of the year, 43 to 40.

The same reporters, who had given us only perfunctory attention after the Hull game, were now climbing all over each other to get to the Roland dressing room. In their stories the following morning, they referred to the Roland team as "Giant Killers" and "Nerveless Norwegians with ice water in their veins". It was great copy. There is nothing Americans love better than when the lowly conquer the mighty. Especially, when the leader of such a victory is a five-foot-six-inch fifteen-year-old boy!

On Friday evening, the night after the West Waterloo game, the Rockets went up against East Des Moines. The question everyone was asking was, "Can Roland do it again?" The conventional wisdom again said no. According to the experts, the Rockets had played way over their heads against West Waterloo and were bound to have a let down. It was asking too much to expect the smallest team in the tournament to defeat the tallest. No, East Des Moines was bound to win and probably by a substantial margin.

The Roland players took to the floor, and the capacity crowd stood and roared. There was no doubt whom the fans were for! This had an adverse effect on the East Des Moines boys, who seemed edgy and nervous during their pre-game warm-up. The Rockets, on the other hand, appeared almost matter-of-fact about the approaching game.

The opening whistle blew, and East Des Moines controlled the ball. Like the previous game, East Des Moines took an early lead. But, for some unexplained reason, they let Gary Thompson shoot his long, one-handed push shot. Every time he hit, he brought fans to their feet. And every basket chipped away at the confidence of the East Des Moines team. Early in the second half, Roland took the lead and control. The fourth quarter was all Rockets. Final score: Roland 46, East Des Moines 37.

The secret to the relatively easy win over East Des Moines

was an almost perfectly played defensive game. Time after time the Rockets confined the much larger team to one off balance shot at the basket. The play of the front court on the defensive board was magnificent. There was no fluke about the victory over East Des Moines. Roland proved to those who still doubted that it was a disciplined, well coached basketball team that belonged in the championship game.

The title was on the line the following evening against the Davenport Blue Devils. Davenport was the largest school in the state, claiming over two thousand students. Roland had eighty-five. Also, the Blue Devils had won more state championships than any other school. It was Roland's first time in the tournament. There was no question who the entire state (the city of Davenport excepted) was rooting for. I doubt if any one high school basketball game in Iowa has ever gained so much attention. The game was front page news in the *Des Moines Register*. Even people who normally did not follow basketball were interested to see if the "Might Mites" from Roland could defeat the "Kings" from Davenport.

Davenport jumped off to an early lead, but like West Waterloo and East Des Moines, it could not break the game open. Roland was again controlling the tempo. The Blue Devils were known for their lightning fast break, and any team that ran with them was sure to lose. So, the Rockets played their usual slow, deliberate game.

The Blue Devils had seen enough of Gary Thompson to realize his long range shooting was for real. One of them had a hand in front of Gary's face all night. But, even though Gary was getting most of the press, Roland was not a one man team. The other four picked up the slack and hit their shots.

The Rocket defense was nearly perfect. By denying the Blue Devils, their fast break, Roland forced them to shoot from the outside. This was not their style, and it showed on the scoreboard. The margin between the two teams diminished, and the frustration of the Davenport players increased. They began forcing long passes, which were promptly intercepted by Don Holland and Gary Thompson. Each of those mistakes usually put two more points on the Roland side of the board.

Halfway through the fourth quarter, Roland took the lead. The noise in the field house was something that had to be heard to be appreciated. Paul Moon, the coach of the Blue Devils, called a time out. I felt sure we were going to win!

I was wrong.

For the Cinderella team from Roland Consolidated, midnight came with two minutes and fifty-nine seconds showing on the University of Iowa clock. For whatever reason, the tremendous poise the Roland team had shown throughout the tournament cracked. The Rockets lost control of the game's tempo and began to run with the Blue Devils. Within a minute-and-a-half, Davenport had scored ten points and put the game out of reach. It all happened so fast that the fans sat stunned a the buzzer. The final score: Davenport 50, Roland 40. For those of us from Roland, there was a feeling of sadness coupled with great pride. Davenport may have won the championship, but Roland had captured the hearts of the Iowa population.

Considering the size of Roland Consolidated, its athletic records border on the phenomenal. The school competed in state tournament play seven times in boys' basketball, three times in girls' basketball, six times in baseball, and six times in girls' softball. Championships were won in boys' basketball and girls' softball.

One of the things about the school that fascinates my non-Roland friends is how I was able to take part in so many different extra curricular activities. My senior year, for example, I played basketball and baseball (poorly), performed in the band, sang in the chorus, boys' glee club, mixed quartet, and madrigal, and had the lead in the senior play. And to the surprise of my friends, this schedule was not exceptional. I can think of five of my classmates who were equally busy. Did our academics suffer? Probably, to some extent. I certainly should have studied more. But the graduates of RHS seem to have done all right for themselves. In my class, all of the boys and many of the girls have some college training. There are eight or nine bachelor degrees, at least four master degrees, and one CPA. The school must have taught us something.

The Roland community loved its school, but it became progressively more difficult to maintain the quality of education desired. During the 1960's, the costs increased to a point where it became necessary to combine with another school. So, in 1969, the school district voted to combine with that of neighboring Story City. A proud tradition ended. Anyone who graduated from Roland Consolidated felt a loss. Our feelings were best expressed in a poem written by my brother, Pete. It isn't great poetry, but not bad for an Iowa hog farmer.

The End of An Era

I saw an era end this night,
A night I knew must come,
But the heart is a bit more stubborn
To accept progress's total sum.
I watched the colors black and red
Leave the court, their final bye;
My heart bled just a mite,
'Twas the end of Roland High.
My thoughts flew back to many years
Before I wore the colors,
To the early "stars" of Roland High,
The bloomer gals and their big, strong fellers.
Then came the '40s and the '50s,
A dynasty emerged.
A name to be feared by other towns,
A greated spirit surged.
"Super Stars" wore the black and red,
Put Roland on the map;
The crowds were big, the fans fantastic
For every game on tap.
Still the colors go on to further glory,
For time cannot stand still;
Reorganize is the cry - the thing to do -
o ease the till.

JERRY L. TWEDT

That fateful day has now arrived
For Roland High to cease;
The conflict has ended, the race been run;
Black and Red may rest in peace.
Back to reality my thoughts were jarred,
The bleachers nearly bared.
With "Roland High" ringing in my ears,
Had others my thoughts shared?
Yes, Roland High, we'll sing to you
Of great times old and new.
For the honor was mine to walk your halls,
My heart will be with you.

✒ The War

December 7, 1941 was a day of infamy; a day that shattered the tranquility of our nation; a day that set into motion the creation of the most powerful war machine the world had ever known; a day of which I have absolutely no recollection. I have no vivid memories of relatives clustered around the radio, talking in hushed tones and listening for the latest bulletins. No matter how I try, I can recall no ashen faces, angry oaths, or tears. The only importance the day had for me was that it brought Christmas one day closer.

As it did to the entire country, the war brought abrupt and wrenching changes to Central Iowa. Many young men quit their jobs and enlisted in the service. Others, like my Uncle Virgil Twedt and cousins, Harold and Vern Jacobson, were drafted. Women, who had been carefully planning June weddings, were either forced to say "I do" in December of January, or to postpone their marital plans indefinitely. Parents and wives found themselves lying awake nights worrying about what was happening to their sons and husbands in such places as Fort Leonard Wood, Fort Riley, and the Great Lakes Naval Base.

The war became the central fact of life within the adult

Top Junk Gatherers: Left to Right:
Jerry Twedt, Gary Thompson, Everett Sather, Wally Frandsen

world. However, to a six-year-old boy, in the first grade of Roland Consolidated school, it was remote and insignificant. I was much too busy learning to write my name and reading about the adventures of Dick, Jane, and Tags to be concerned about what was happening in Europe and Asia. Like most six year olds, I didn't even know the two continents existed. Even the coming of sugar and gas rationing failed to make the war seem real or important. Mother was still able to make great cookies, and my Shetland pony required no gasoline.

It wasn't until the fall of 1942 that the war began to make an impression on me. My awakening to the struggle began when I discovered that the eraser on my pencil was no longer attached with a metal strip, and that the eraser left heavy black marks. I asked Miss Cunningham, my second grade teacher, why we could no longer buy good erasers attached with metal strips? She informed me that all metal and rubber were going to the war effort. About this time, I also learned that it was no longer possible to buy Wrigley's Spearmint gum. Again, the answer was the war. By taking away my favorite gum and rubber erasers, World War II had finally penetrated my small world.

We all tried to do our part for the war effort. My older brother Pete's class crocheted squares that were made into blankets. Now, what the army did with crocheted blankets, I'll never know. But the seventh graders, at Roland Consolidated, were crocheting their hearts out. We all bought ten cent war stamps. Each week we would buy one and stick it in our stamp books. If we were diligent and did not spend the dime for pop or candy, we were able to trade the full stamp book in for a war bond. Strange as it may seem, very few of those dimes went for anything but stamps. We all had relatives who were soldiers, and spending the money on ourselves was like stealing from them.

My involvement in the war effort began when, in order to help alleviate the critical need for steel, the first six grades of our school had a junk drive. Each teacher was given a large cardboard box, and we were asked to try and fill it. To give the drive a competitive atmosphere, each student's offerings were to be weighed, and a prize was to be given in each class to the child who brought in the most junk. Also, there was an overall prize to be given to the outstanding class.

The teachers and superintendent completely underestimated the response and the amount of junk in and around Roland! Within a few days, our box was overflowing, and we had begun on a second. By the time a week had passed, the entire school was bulging with scrap metal. This was especially true of the sixth grade, where almost every spare inch of space was taken.

The superintendent had no choice but to order all the junk out of the school and put in six separate piles on the schoolyard. This decision really opened the flood gates. We had been limited to small pieces of scrap we could carry. After going outside, our fathers could bring in trailer loads of rusting farm implements. The piles soon swelled with everything from horse drawn gang plows to cook ranges.

The children of Roland Consolidated loved it! We had strict orders not to play on the piles, but telling small boys not to climb on such treasures as old cultivators is like ordering bees to stay away from flowers. We became well acquainted with each grade's pile. My favorite belonged to the sixth grade. It was the biggest and had, near the bottom, an old gang plough. I discovered I could wiggle my way down to the plow and sit on the seat. It was like being inside of a real tank! If I were quiet, nobody knew I was in there. But I was seldom quiet. It is very difficult to shoot down a million Zeroes and Messerschmitts without yelling.

My diligent gleaning allowed me to be one of the top gatherers in our class. There were four of us in the running for the prize, but, to my knowledge, the award was never given. I think the large pieces delivered by our fathers caused Miss Cunningham to lose track of who had brought what. She did, however, take a photograph of us sitting in front of the boxes of scrap. The picture, still a prized possession, reveals four very proud little boys.

The excitement I experienced because of the contest, plus the pride I felt in being one of the winners, created a fascination with the war. I began to follow the progress of our armies closely by listening to the radio newscasts. One only had to follow my play to know where the action was. I first built an orange crate airplane and flew with the Flying Tigers. No Zero stood a chance against my shark-faced P-40! Even if I had known that the Flying Tigers ceased to exist as a fighting unit when we entered the war, it would have made no difference. Facts are unimportant when you are seven. After flying the P-40, I joined the Marines and fought my way through the jungles of Guadalcanal. For weeks, I went around singing the first two lines of the Marine Hymn. Next I was transferred to North Africa where I fought alongside of Montgomery. I even had my own tank! To some unimaginative adult, it was an empty fifty gallon drum sitting in an old oats wagon, but to me, it was a Sherman, capable of destroying the whole Africa Corps! I, of course, landed at Normandy, flew countless B-17 missions over Germany, and, in my spare time, made commando raids. What is more, I accomplished all of this after school and on Saturdays. I didn't think it proper to play war on Sunday.

Although I listened to the news programs, my image of the war was shaped largely by movies and the children's radio programs. This image was clear and sharply focused. World War II was a fight between good and evil, a gigantic morality play in which the forces of light battled the powers of darkness. There was no subtlety of shading. The Americans were the good guys in the white hats, whereas the Germans and the Japs were villains. The American soldier was the complete antitheses of his German and Japanese counterparts. He was brave and courageous, yet kind to animals and gentle with children. There was a clean cut quality about him that was visualized by Norman Rockwell on the covers of *The Saturday Evening Post*. He had a clear eye, a strong chin, a pure heart, and never said a cuss word more profane than "darn"! He was Davy Crockett, Paul Bunyon, and St. Paul rolled into one.

Above all else, the American soldier was invincible. This I accepted as a simple fact of life; so did every other youngster I knew. Who could believe differently after seeing such movies as "Destination Tokyo", "So Proudly We Hail", or "Purple Heart". There were times in these films when all looked lost, but at the moment of crisis, John Wayne or Alan Ladd or whatever star it happened to be, would rally the troops and lead them to glorious victory! The Story City Theatre would erupt with cheers. We would stomp our feet and scream, "Get 'em!" This was what we had come to see. Enacted before our eyes, with the accompaniment of a full orchestra, was the unconquerable American soldier blazing his way through the enemy ranks. Nothing and no one could stop him!

Attending these war movies was somewhat like going to communion. We came out of the theatre with our faith renewed and more convinced than ever of America's invincibility in battle. Our convictions were evident in our flushed, excited faces. We pointed our fingers and shot hordes of Germans and Japanese; we darted into doorways and threw imaginary hand grenades; and we talked of what we would do if we were "over there". All of us were miniature John Waynes, secretly hoping the war would last long enough for us to get a crack at the enemy.

Just as important as the movies in forming my concept of American invincibility, were the children's radio programs. Monday through Friday, from five until six in the afternoon, the radio super heroes fought the Nazis and Japs with amazing success. At five o'clock came "Hop Harrigan", which was followed at five-fifteen by "Jack Armstrong, the All American Boy". Then at five-thirty, "Captain Midnight" swooped across the radio sky.

Of the three, my favorite was "Hop Harrigan". He, along

with his sidekick, "Tank Tinker", fought the whole German Luftwaffe to a standstill. Not only that! He also went on secret missions behind enemy lines and accepted assignments that lesser men refused. I remember vividly the exciting conclusion of one such adventure.

Hop and Tank were on a secret mission deep in Germany. Their assignment was to blow up a factory which had been built inside of a mountain. The two had worked their way into the factory, had set the time charges, and were making their escape when they were discovered. Shots were fired! Tank fell wounded! What would happen? Would they be captured? Was this the end of the great flying ace and his faithful friend? Tune in tomorrow, same time, same station for...Hop Harrigan!

I bit my nails for the next twenty-four hours. When it came time for the program, I put my ear next to the radio speaker and breathlessly waited. The Germans were shooting at my two heroes. By some stroke of luck, an airplane was being warmed up right there in the factory! Hop helped his wounded pal into the single-seater plane and squeezed in himself. All the while, machine gun bullets were whizzing all around Hop and Tank. (It is no wonder we won the war. The Germans were lousy shots!!) Hop pushed in the throttle and roared toward the mountain opening. As he did, he saw the great steel doors begin to close! Would Hop make it through before the doors closed? Would the charges go off before he was clear of the mountain? No! They wouldn't do it to me again! Oh, yes they would! It was "tune in tomorrow" for you know what.

For another twenty-four hours I fretted over my heroes.

When Hop again hit the airwaves, he was still hurtling toward the closing steel doors. He gave the plane full throttle and took off while still inside the mountain! There seemed no hope he could make it through the rapidly closing space between the two doors, but Hop skillfully tilted his wings and flew through at an angle! He then pulled back on the stick and climbed up and over the surrounding mountain peaks. Just as he made it up into the safety of the sky, the entire mountain housing the factory blew up! Hop had won again! He flew Tank back to a hospital, where it was discovered that his friend only had a flesh wound. I knew then that come Monday (all climaxes to stories came on Friday) Hop and Tank would be off on a new adventure.

These serials took on an added dimension when they offered a special gift. All a child had to do was send in twenty-five cents in coin (no stamps, please), plus one box top from the sponsor's cereal, and within a few weeks, he would be the proud owner of whatever was offered. Through this process, I acquired spurs, decoders, badges, secret compartment rings (they never worked), and a cardboard model of a B-17 Flying Fortress.

Though we had little money, Mother always seemed to be able to find the necessary quarter or fifty cents to enable me to order my latest heart's desire. The only times she balked, was when she knew I did not like the product from which I needed the box top or label. When these situations arose, the scene was played as follows:

Mother

(Firmly)
No! you don't like that!

Me

(With wide-eyed astonishment)
What? Sure I do.

Mother

You do not! Neither do the other kids. The last time I bought
it, I had to throw it out!

Me

But I like it now! Please, Mom! I promise I'll eat it! I
promise!

Mother

That's what you said last time.

Me

This time is different! I'll eat it! Oh, please, Mom, I just gotta'
have the ....! All of my friends are getting one!

51

JERRY L. TWEDT

Mother

(Not so firmly)
Well, I don't think so.

After a few more days of playing the same scene over and over again, Mother would reluctantly put the product on her shopping list. However, she then took a rather sadistic pleasure in making me eat or drink the detested stuff!

A good example of this was a chocolate powder called Ovaltine. For some reason, I hated it! The problem was that Ovaltine sponsored "Captain Midnight", a program that featured secret messages. At the end of each program, Captain Midnight would use a number code to send the message. Unless you had the decoder, there was no way of translating the communication. To add to the problem, a new decoder was offered every few months. This, of course, meant another jar of Ovaltine. However, Mother would not buy a new jar until I finished the nearly full one sitting on the pantry shelf. If I really wanted the decoder, I had no choice, but to go on an Ovaltine binge. However, the decoder was worth it. I remember sitting at the kitchen table pretending I was a secret agent receiving instructions through the B.B.C. The message was something like "Loose lips sink ships", or "Soldiers drink Ovaltine, too". Whatever the message, the decoding was the fun part.

I also had fun with a B-17 bomber I received from the "Hop Harrigan" program. The bomb bay consisted of a circular disk which held marbles. There was a hole in the bottom of the plane, and as the disk was turned, the marbles fell through the opening. To line up your target, you looked in the tail of the plane at a mirror angled so that you could see the floor. As a bonus, small paper ships, which served as targets, were sent with the plane. I loved that airplane, but as it was constructed of heavy paper, it didn't last long. Neither did the ships. In making my bombing runs, I usually ended up stepping on them.

The most popular offering by a radio program actually took place following the war. It was the Atom Bomb Ring! Oddly enough, "The Lone Ranger", was the show that offered it. What the atom bomb had to do with the wild west, I will never know. Perhaps, the sponsor just knew a good thing when he saw it.

The ring consisted of a metallic blue "Bomb", with a red plastic guide fin cap, attached to an adjustable band. The bomb was set high on the band, so it was impossible to wear gloves or mittens and the ring at the same time. Since my friends and I received our rings in the middle of winter, this was a problem. There were just two alternatives: take the ring off, which none of us wanted to do, or run around with one cold hand. For a week, most of the boys in elementary school had one cold hand!

The reason for all the excitement was that you were supposed to be able to see actual atoms bouncing off each other. All you had to do was go into a dark room, take off the plastic cap and stare into the back of the bomb. In school, the only dark place was the janitor's broom closet, which was located in the boy's bathroom. For about a week, during the noon hour, the bathroom was packed with boys waiting in line for their turn in the broom closet. When a boy came out of the closet, he was asked by all if he had seen anything. The boy replied the equivalent of, "Yeah! Wow! Gee! It's great!" After my turn, I said something similar. To be honest, however, I never saw a blooming thing! And I bet that none of the other guys did either. It was a classic example of the "Emperor's New Clothes". Each of us was unwilling to admit that his atom bomb ring didn't work!

Until the summer of 1944, my moralistic, stereotyped thinking on the war remained intact. Then two events happened that initiated me into the true realities of war.

The first occurred when the Marshall Canning Company began to can sweet corn. Because of the manpower shortage, German prisoners of war were brought in so that the plant could run at full capacity.

I wanted to see the POW's, but at the same time was frightened by the prospect. My chance came when Dad drove to the factory to see when his corn would be picked. As we traveled to town, all sorts of wild thoughts passed through my mind. What if there should be an escape while I was there? What if I were taken hostage? What should I do if there was shooting? I suddenly wished I had stayed home. The killer of thousands of imaginary Nazis was scared to death of meeting a real German soldier.

Dad parked the car by the office and went in. I was right on his heels. While Dad conducted his business,, I stared out of the window at the prisoners, who were standing at ease in ranks outside the factory. They were wearing blue work pants and blue shirts with P O W painted in large white numbers on the back. I thought I saw one of the soldiers look at me, and I jumped back from the window. When I looked again, the men had broken ranks and were walking toward the factory. As I watched, I felt a growing sense of disappointment. There wasn't a shaved head or a monocle in the bunch. Not one of them looked like a vicious mad dog. They all appeared so..so..normal. They looked just like the Roland boys, who had gone off to war to fight them.

Once Dad finished talking to the manager, he and I crossed over to the factory and looked in on the huge canning room. Instead of gaping at the machines, which was what I usually did, I looked for the prisoners. To my surprise, they were not in a group, but scattered about the room working right along side the local people. In many cases, the locals and the prisoners were not only working together, they were also talking to each other! I especially noticed one teenage girl, who was putting cans into boxes. She and the prisoner beside her were laughing so hard they could hardly work. Then, another woman offered half of a sandwich to the German next to her. I was shocked. This was no way to treat the enemy!

On the way home, Dad saw that I was upset. "What's the matter, Jerry?"

"Those women were laughing and talking with the Germans!"

"What's wrong with that?" Dad asked.

I could not believe my ears. Didn't Dad understand? "They are the enemy!"

Dad did not say anything for a moment, then sort of shook his head. "Yes, they are, but they're still people."

The thought of Germans and Japanese being people was as shocking as the woman sharing her sandwich. In my play, they had always been the cruel, faceless enemy. My father's simple statement, plus actually seeing German soldiers, made me realize that war was people fighting people. My simple, moralistic view of war began to crack.

The view totally collapsed when, a few weeks later, my family was notified that Uncle Virgil had been killed in action. Although I had been aware that he was fighting in France, the thought of his dying never crossed my mind. Virgil was a good guy. In my neat, imaginary war, only bad guys died. Good guys might get wounded a little, but they always lived to come home to a hero's welcome. Virgil's death exploded that myth.

Virgil was an unlikely soldier. He was a friendly, happy-go-lucky fellow, who had no quarrel with anyone. Pointing a gun at a fellow human being and killing him was completely foreign to his character. Virgil must have sensed his poor aptitude for soldiering. He told my father that if he ever went overseas, he would never come back. He was right.

Before being drafted, Virgil's life was settled and happy. He had married his high school sweetheart, Alice Ritland, bought a home, and owned a truck-mounted grinding mill. The farmers, around Roland, knew and liked Virgil, so his red-cab truck was on the go most of the time. He had the prospects for making a good living.

My personal memories of Virgil are meager. I was just beginning to get to know him when he was drafted. My one vivid recollection illustrates his fun-loving nature.

I was six years old, and for some forgotten reason, I was spending the day with my Aunt Alice. It was hot day, and I was impatiently waiting for the afternoon to come because I had been promised a swim in the Erickson Park wading pool. Lunch time arrived. Virgil and a young man he had helping him, came laughing through the front door. Since both were covered with grinding dust, they yelled hello to Alice and went up the stairs to wash up.

When the men came downstairs, the hired man took off his shirt and stretched out, face down, on the cool dining room linoleum. As for Virgil, he went into the kitchen to say hello to his new bride. When he returned an saw his hired man lying on the floor, he looked for a moment, then a devilish smile spread across his handsome face. He darted back into the kitchen and returned with a steaming baked potato wrapped in a hot pad holder. He put his finger to his lips for me to be quiet, then flipped the potato on to the hired man's back. The man yelled and leaped to his feet. Virgil roared with laughter. After realizing what Virgil had done, the man attempted to pick up the potato and chase Virgil. But, the potato was too hot to handle, and it bounced across the dining room floor. By this time, Alice was on the scene and put an end to the antics. I loved it! I didn't know big people had that much fun.

Virgil's fun ended on the hedgerows of France. His death caused Alice to go from a vivacious young girl to a heartbroken widow. Her one consolation was my cousin Allen, who had been born just before Virgil shipped out.

After the war, Virgil's body was brought back and re-buried in the Roland Cemetery. There was the bronze casket, the flag, the salute of rifles, and the playing of "Taps". It was very solemn and very impressive. But, when I remember Virgil, I choose to forget the soldier. I prefer to recall a young man bent over with laughter at a prank he had just pulled on a friend. This was the real Virgil Twedt.

Virgil's death did not end my imaginary "daring do". I remained an avid fan of Hop Harrigan and John Wayne. However, the reality of war was much more sharply focused. I became very aware of the gold stars hanging in the windows of too many Roland homes. I then realized that every gold star represented a Virgil Twedt, who would never again play a prank, kiss his bride, or watch his son grow into manhood.

During the spring of 1945, our troops, in the best Hollywood tradition, charged across Germany and left the Third Reich in ashes. A few months later the Enola Gay dropped atomic death on Hiroshima, and, within days, World War II was over. Our victorious soldiers returned to the sound of trumpets and the cheers of the entire nation. We had defeated the that tyrants! The world was at peace. No one realized how short peace was to be.

❧ Tony

Ahorse was much more to a farm boy than just something to ride. He was a partner in countless hold-ups and shoot-outs, one's only means of escape from bloody Indian raids, and the winner of hundreds of Kentucky Derbies. He had a chameleon-like ability, no matter what size or color, to become Trigger, Champion, Topper, or even the great horse, Silver. A horse was also a confidant of one's deepest secrets and wildest dreams, and a friend who dribbled water on one's head when sharing a drink. He was a cunning adversary who caused tears of frustration to flow when he would not allow himself to be bridled. And, perhaps, most of all, he was a means of escaping the farm yard and breaking free of parental restraint. He, in short, was an indispensable colleague in those blurred years of reality and fantasy we call childhood.

My personal love affair with the horse began when my cousin, Harlan Hall, was given a pony. I think I was almost as excited as he was. It didn't matter that the pony was one of the world's most miserable excuses for an equine. Whoever had owned it before my Uncle Si and Aunt Irene must not have cared for the poor little pinto at all. The poor thing was a

Tony, ridden by my cousin, Orlan Branjord.

walking skeleton. Because of its sharp backbone, riding at a trot was unbearable. But, no matter, I was as envious as any five-year-old can get and began immediately to badger Mother and Dad for a pony.

To make matters worse, within a period of weeks, my cousin, David Twedt, received a pony. Her name was Daisy. She was an old, reddish-brown Shetland with a shaggy mane and tail and the spirit of a burned-out draft horse. Although she wasn't much, she could be ridden and hitched to an ancient buggy owned by Uncle Leonard. David had a world of fun with her. All of this made my need for a pony that much greater. Mother and Dad received no rest. All I could think or talk about was a pony! Their answer was always the same. "We'll see when your birthday comes."

With the exception of my army basic training, the weeks leading to my sixth birthday were undoubtedly the slowest of my life. I had never wanted anything so much as a pony. The days seemed to drag by as if they were carried on the backs of turtles. Anyone who has ever wanted something so badly that the thought of not getting it was too painful to endure, knows how I felt.

Finally, July 3, 1941, arrived. I awoke to see the morning sun filling the room. I jumped out of bed, threw on my clothes, and charged down the stairs. Somehow, on this day of days, I had overslept.

We had a tradition, in our family, of receiving birthday presents at breakfast, and, as I ran into the kitchen, the entire family was gathered around the table. There were some packages on my chair, and Mother had made pancakes. But, I wasn't interested in food or packages.

"Happy Birthday, Jerry!" They all said in unison.

Without even bothering to say thank you, I ran full tilt for the back door. I dashed out into the yard, my heart pounding and a triumphant yell just waiting to be born. I had imagined this scene a thousand times.

Nothing.

I looked behind the trees, the shrubs, and even under the porch. There was no pony. I froze for a moment, not willing to believe what my eyes told me. Then I thought of the front yard. The pony must be there! My hopes soared a I ran around the house.

No pony.

As I stared at the empty front yard, I couldn't believe that I had not received my pony. I had been so sure...so very sure. My triumphant yell died and swelled in my throat. Great tears began pouring from my eyes.

"Come in and eat, Jerry," Dad called. "Your pancakes are getting cold."

I didn't care if they were getting cold. The truth was, I didn't care about anything. Slowly, I made my way into the kitchen, moved my packages, and sat down. I made no effort to hide my disappointment or my tears. No one said much. Mother poured some hot syrup on my pancakes and urged me to eat. I took a few bites, but was far too upset to eat my usual number of pancakes. I just sat there and let my salty tears fall onto my plate and mix with the sweet syrup.

"Aren't you going to open your presents?" My eight-year-old sister Herma asked.

I picked up the gaily wrapped packages and began to take off the paper. I couldn't have cared less about opening them. There was no way of wrapping what I wanted.

After I opened my gifts (I have no idea what was in those boxes.), Dad got up from the table and told my brother, Pete, who was eleven to get ready to go with him to town.

"Can I go along?" I asked.

"No," Dad said. "You'd better stay home."

Denying me the chance to go to town was more than I could take, and I loosed a fresh supply of tears. At that moment, I was the saddest birthday boy in the state of Iowa.

After Dad and Pete left, I stomped around the house with the longest face ever. My disappointment turned to cold anger. I glared at my mother and sister and thought to myself how I would run away from home and never come back! Then they would be sorry I hadn't been given my pony!

Mother must not have been able to stand any more sorrowful looks from her little boy, because she gave me a kiss and whispered, "Your birthday isn't over yet." I asked her what she meant by that, but she said no more. She just smiled in a mysterious way and went about her work.

Like the mythical phoenix, hope was reborn. I rushed down to the road and impatiently waited for Dad to return. Perhaps I would get my pony after all! I even dared to daydream again.

When my pony arrived, I would jump on his back and together we would race down the road, the wind blowing in our faces! He would be the most beautiful pony in the world. He also would be the fastest and the smartest. He would happily obey every command, and most of all, he would love me as much as I loved him.

Finally, I saw our black 1935 Ford come into view. It was traveling very slowly, so I ran out into the road to see why. There, trotting along beside the car, was a black pony!

My yell of triumph was born! I continued to shout as I dashed for the house. Mother and Herma came out from the kitchen as I reached the porch.

"Dad's got a pony!" I yelled. "He's got a pony!"

Mother smiled and said, "Are you sure it's for you? Maybe Sue's pony has run away again."

Thud!

I was back down on earth. Our neighbor girl had a black pony, which was constantly running away. Mother saw the look on my face and laughed. There was a gleam in her eyes, and I knew at that moment my birthday wish was about to come true.

His name was Tony. He was a Shetland, and as he trotted up the drive, his coal black hide glistened. My daydreams had come true! He was the most beautiful pony in the world. At first glance, his fine, almost delicate features and tiny hooves made him seem fragile, but on closer inspection, one saw the strong legs and powerful muscles that propelled him up to speeds of thirty miles per hour.

"He can really go!" Pete said, as he jumped out of the car and onto Tony's back.

Pete galloped Tony around the farm yard, and everyone, especially me, was impressed with the pony's speed. He was everything I dreamed of and more.

I learned later that Tony loved to race, and because of his ability to be running at full speed after only a couple of strides, he was nearly unbeatable in a short race. However, in any long race, the larger horses would pass him. He hated this! Any time a horse went by, he flattened his ears against his head and tried to take a nip out of the faster animal. I had to be on the lookout for this, because, at times, he came awfully close to getting the leg of the boy who was riding the other horse.

"Let me ride!" I begged.

Pete rode Tony up to where I was standing and jumped off. I petted Tony and noticed that the top half of his mane lay to the left and bottom half to the right. In the years that followed, I discovered that no amount of currying or brushing made it lie any other way.

That magic moment had arrived! I took the reins in my hands, and Dad lifted me onto Tony's back. For a time, I just sat there. I was too happy to do anything else. For me, it was one of those few interludes of pure joy that is granted in a lifetime.

"Make him go!" Pete said.

I tightened my grip on the reins and kicked Tony in the ribs. "Get up, Tony!"

Tony didn't move.

"Get up! Get up, Tony!" I commanded again.

Tony stood there as if he were deaf and I didn't even exist!

"Get up, Tony!" I shouted and again kicked him in the ribs. For good measure, I added an unauthoritative slap of the reins that wouldn't have hurt my baby brother!

Tony moved, but in the wrong direction. He backed up! Everyone laughed.

"You're going to have to show him who's boss," Dad said.

The problem was that Tony knew perfectly well who was boss. That's why he wasn't moving forward.

Dad finally gave Tony a sharp slap on the rump, and he started off for the barn at a quick trot. I stayed with him for at least twenty feet before we parted company. Again everyone laughed. I didn't care. To my family, I was sitting on the ground, but in reality, I was sitting on top of the world.

For the next three years, Tony was both companion and tormentor. I spilled many tears proving to him, "who was boss". Like most Shetlands, Tony was cunning, resourceful, and lazy. Unlike so many of his breed, he was good tempered and gentle. It was perfectly safe for a child to crawl through his legs, pull his mane, or hang onto his tail. I never knew him to kick at a human. He only tried to bite when losing a race.

Our relationship, however, turned out to be very one-sided. I loved him. He tolerated me. On his part, there was none of the honey-coated warmth one finds in so many horse stories written for children. To him, I was just another crazy kid who made him run all over the countryside chasing imaginary outlaws and Indians. If I fell off and dropped the reins, he headed for home at a full gallop. If I only wanted to pet him and had no oats to offer as a bribe, he ignored me. And if I put my arms around him to give him a hug, he just pushed me away. Tony was the most independent animal on the farm. In a way, it was a shame he wasn't born in the wild. His need for human attention or affection was, at the most, minimal.

I had two major problems with Tony that first year: catching him, and making him go. The first dilemma I solved by tempting him with a pan of oats. As I moved closer, I would also tell him lies like, "I don't want to ride you, Tony. I just want to give you some oats." He looked at me with unmasked disdain, not the least taken in by my words; but because of his love for oats, he stood his ground. Once he was eating, I edged closer and closer until I was near enough to lunge and grab him around the neck. Then, all that remained was to put on the bridle, which I had hidden from Tony's view by sticking it down the back of my pants. I always felt a pleasant sense of victory after the capture was completed.

Solving the problem of making him go, was not so easily accomplished. I kicked, slapped, yelled, and cried; but if Tony decided not to obey, he either backed up or turned in a tight circle. I shed more tears over making Tony go where I wanted, when I wanted, than over any other single cause. During the first few months, this stubborn attitude rewarded him by restricting my area of travel to the farm yard. But, the following spring, it earned him one of the wildest rides of his life.

My Uncle Leslie Twedt, a tall, handsome man in his early thirties, was at our farm planting corn. About three-thirty, one afternoon, Mother gave me a jar of cold water and a small lunch bag containing a sandwich and homemade cookies, and sent me off on Tony to the field. With even the slightest cooperation from Tony, I should have taken no more than ten minutes to reach where Les was planting. I took nearly thirty!

Tony was in one of his moods, and, being fully aware that my hands were occupied with the jar and lunch, and thus unable to slap him with the reins, he refused to budge. All I could do was kick. And kick I did! But Tony just laid back his ears and stood there, challenging me to do something. I felt like hitting him in the head with a two by four, but instead, I did the sensible thing...I called Mother. With her aid, we pointed Tony in the right direction, and, as Pete used to say, "I was off like a herd of turtles!"

The ride out to Les was a struggle of pride and will power. It would have been much quicker for me to jump off and walk, but I wasn't about to give in to that mule-headed pony. I had learned that if I were to ride Tony, I had to out stubborn him. I yelled, kicked, cried, and even swore a little. Tony responded with a glacial walk.

After what seemed an hour, my route finally intersected the path of the planter. Les pulled old Dick and Dave to a halt.

"Whoa!" he said, grinning at the angry, disgusted look on my face. He was planting on a hill and had been in position to see the entire war.

"What took you so long?" he asked, getting off of the planter and taking the food and water from me.

"I couldn't make this dumb old pony go!" I answered.

"What's the matter? Can't you ride?"

"I can ride!" I said defensively. "I just can't make him go!"

Les laughed and ate his sandwich. I waited glumly for him to finish. Tony stood placidly, waiting to do what he wanted all along, go home.

"So, you can't make him go, huh?" Les said after finishing the sandwich and taking a long drink of water.

"No." I muttered.

Les took out his pliers and cut off two lengths of spare planter wire. "Well, I think it's time that pony of yours learned a lesson."

"What are you going to do?"

"You'll see," Les said, taking Tony by the bridle. "Get off and hold the horses."

I jumped off Tony and crawled up onto the planter seat where I picked up the reins. It really wasn't necessary. Dick and Dave would have loved nothing better than to stand in one spot the rest of their lives.

Les took Tony's reins in one hand, and with the planter wire in the other, he swung onto Tony's back. Now, Les was over six feet tall and his feet nearly dragged on the ground. The sight of big Les sitting on little Tony was the stuff that made the Keystone Cops so hilarious.

It was funny to me, but not to Tony. He was one surprised little horse! "Get up!" Les shouted, and wrapped the planting wire around the pony's belly. Tony's legs were a blur of motion. By starting so fast, he almost caused Les to fall off! Les regained his balance and rode Tony in a large circle over the unplanted land. I had never seen Tony move so fast. And whenever he began to slow down, Les hit him with the planter wire. This went on for several minutes. When Les brought Tony back to the planter, my stubborn little pony had been transformed into a sweating, wild-eyed bundle of nerves.

"There!" Les said with satisfaction as he got off of Tony. "That ought to make him think twice."

Les took a long drink from the jar, then lifted me onto Tony and handed me the jar. "Thank your mother for the lunch." He said, and slapped Tony on the rump.

Tony broke for home with a burst of speed that made me drop the jar and grab onto his mane. Coming out I couldn't make him move. Going home, I couldn't make him stop! What a ride! At first, I was convinced I would fall off and kill myself. But as the ride continued, my body caught the rhythm of Tony's stride, and I began to relax. My fear turned to excitement. This was what I had dreamed about! By the time we reached the farmyard, Tony had run himself out, and I was in full control. I entered the farmyard like a knight coming home from a victorious battle. Tony was never again able to bully me.

With my new found self-assurance, I even learned to harness him and hook him to the cart. Tony liked being driven less than being ridden, so he always fought going between the shafts of the pony cart. His favorite trick was to step out of the shafts, before I had a chance to pick them up and put them through the harness loops. The best way to beat this was to have Herma or Pete help me, but if they weren't around, I put the shafts up on blocks so that once Tony was inside, he found it much more difficult to step out. One way or another, I managed to get him hitched.

My favorite destination, once I had Tony on the road and moving, was Uncle Leonard Twedt's farm. Tony could easily beat my cousin David's pony, Daisy, in a race. Both Tony and I enjoyed this. But about a year after I received Tony, Leonard sold old Daisy and bought David a beautiful black pony mare named Beauty. She was larger than Tony and had a much sweeter disposition. And, oh how she could run! I can't remember a time that Tony beat her from a scratch start. The races were close, but Beauty always won by about a length.

David also had a cart. It had high wooden wheels and, although not as pretty as mine, was lighter. My cart had red wheels, a yellow seat and red shafts, but the wheels were from an old Model T Ford, which added a great deal of weight. When we raced, the heavier cart was a distinct disadvantage to Tony. However, David gave me a slight head start, which evened things out.

There was nothing scientific about those races. The strategy consisted of making our ponies run as hard as possible. I half stood, half sat, slapping Tony with the end of the reins, and all the while screaming for him to go faster! David was doing exactly the same to Beauty. Down the road we'd go, completely oblivious to any danger. For a while the two carts were hub to hub, Ben Hur style, then David pulled ahead. Of course, Tony laid back his ears and did his biting thing, but it never helped. Actually, who won or lost really didn't make much difference. The exhilaration of the race and the combative comradeship it created were what was important.

I had many exciting times with Tony, but only one real adventure. The incident remains vivid in my memory; not only for the danger involved, but because of my stupidity and lack of judgement.

The summer I turned twelve, some of my classmates arranged a big baseball game with the class ahead of us. It was to be held in Roland's Erickson Park, and everybody had to be there. The honor of the class was at stake.

About a half an hour before I planned to leave for town, I was mentally preparing myself for the game by bouncing a ball off our machine shed. As I threw, I dreamed of how I would come up to bat with the bases loaded and hit a game-winning home run. This was always my dream, but it never came close to coming true. I had major league ambition coupled with little league talent.

In my imaginary game, the count was three and two, and I was about to hit the home run, when Mother came out of the house carrying a million quart strawberry boxes. Well, maybe there were only three or four boxes, but it seemed like a million! I explained to her that, due to the big game, picking strawberries was out of the question. She disagreed, whereupon I soon found myself kneeling in amongst the strawberries. I probably had fifteen minutes worth of work to do. But, being a normal lazy kid, I complained and moaned so much, it took me forty-five minutes. When the boxes were finally filled, I ran into the house and dumped them into the sink.

"Thank you, Jerry," Mother said, sweetly.

I said nothing. I just gave her an angry look that I hoped

would send her weeping to her bedroom. It only made her laugh! Humiliated, I ran out the door, jumped on Tony and rode for town.

I had ridden for about a mile and was still boiling when I came to the railroad tracks. It was then I had my great idea. Why not follow the tracks into town! The tracks went near the park and would cut down my ride by a half mile. Since doing this was the only way I could keep from being late, I turned Tony down the tracks.

The first half mile went beautifully. The park was in sight, and I congratulated myself on my brilliant maneuver. Then, to my horror, I was confronted with a large ravine, spanned by a long wooden trestle. Tony stopped dead and refused to take another step.

I could both see and hear the boys warming up. If I went back, it would mean another half hour before I reached the park. A feeling of desperation gripped me. I couldn't go back! I jumped off Tony and began to lead him out onto the trestle. Tony had more sense that I did. He took one step on the trestle and backed off.

"Come on, Tony!" I said. "You can make it!"

Because Tony was so sure-footed, I was convinced he could walk the cross ties. I tugged and pulled, but Tony dug in his front hooves and refused to move. This infuriated me, probably because I knew that he was right in resisting. I jerked hard on the bridle and hit him with the reins.

"Move you dumb horse!"

Tony gave in and gingerly moved onto the trestle. Slowly and carefully we make our way over the cross ties.

"That's it Tony...you're dong great...we'll make it!"

We did not.

Tony's right rear leg missed a cross tie. He lunged forward in a desperate attempt to regain his balance, but only succeeded in driving his forelegs between the ties. Tony's struggle to free himself was magnificent, but brief. In a matter of seconds, he lay helpless on the cross ties.

I stared at Tony in anguished disbelief. How could I have been so stupid! What could I do? There was no way I could help him. I looked around, hoping to see a farmer working one of the surrounding fields. There was no one.

Then I heard it.

At first, I thought I imagined it. But, within moments, the unmistakable sound of a train whistle filled my ears. The Minneapolis and St. Louis freight train was puffing out of Roland and rumbling toward me. I could not believe it. "Old Gooty," as we called the train, only came to Roland twice a week!

Again the whistle sounded. The train was picking up speed. It was then the realization hit me that unless I did something, my pony was going to die. Cold fear paralyzed me as I stood in horror and watched the puffs of smoke coming faster and faster from the engine.

Then, as if released from some giant vise, I began to run!

The train was less than a quarter of a mile away as I raced toward it. I waved my arms and shouted and ran with adrenalin powered speed!

The engineer saw me and whistled angrily for me to get off the tracks. But, I stayed on the tracks and continued to dash toward the train. Again, the engineer blew the whistle, but he also began braking the engine. When I heard the squeal of the brakes and saw the train begin to slow, I jumped to the side of the tracks. My lungs felt as if they were about to burst, and my entire body was trembling.

The engineer ground the hissing locomotive to a stop beside where I was standing. "What the hell you doing, boy?" he bellowed angrily.

"My pony's on the track!" I shouted back.

"What?"

"My pony's stuck on the trestle!"

The engineer gave me a long look, then glanced at the fireman who just shrugged. "All right," the engineer said. "Let's have a look. Get up here!"

The engineer extended his hand, and, before I knew what was happening, I was in the cab of the locomotive. I had dreamed of riding in a steam engine, but now that I had a chance, I was too upset to enjoy it. All I could think of was Tony.

"How'd your pony get on the trestle?" the fireman asked.

"I...I led him on."

"You what?"

"I thought he could walk on the cross ties," I said lamely.

The two men shook their heads and gave me a look that made me feel like the dumbest kid that ever walked.

The locomotive gave a lurch and the train slowly crept

ahead. When we reached the trestle, the engineer eased the locomotive to a halt, and he and the fireman climbed down and crossed to where Tony was stranded. I walked silently behind.

"He's stuck, all right," the fireman said.

"Yep, he sure is," was the engineer's reply.

"Can you get him out?" I asked.

"Well, we're not going anywhere till we do," the engineer muttered. He then turned to the fireman. "You take his head and I'll take his tail. Maybe we can lift him."

The two men grabbed Tony's tail and head and with relatively little difficulty picked him up. As soon as Tony could maneuver, his legs began to scramble. This helped in getting him safely back to solid ground. All three of us quickly began to examine Tony to see if he had been hurt. Outside of some scraped hide, he was fine.

"You're lucky, boy," the engineer said. "He seems to be okay."

"Thank you," I said with a sigh of relief. "Thank you for helping me."

The engineer looked at me and smiled. "You're welcome. But don't let me ever catch you doing a dumb thing like this again."

"You won't!" I blurted. "I promise! I'll never do it again!" I have never said anything I meant more.

The two men laughed, gave Tony a friendly pat, then returned to "Old Gooty" to continue their run. I didn't realize it at the time, but I gave them both a great story to tell their grandchildren.

All of his life, Tony was a reluctant, yet patient teacher. Because of his size, he was constantly introducing young children to the joys of riding. After me, came my brother, Paul. Following Paul, was my sister, Linda. In addition, there were assorted cousins and neighborhood youngsters. About the time Tony thought he was going to get a rest, Pete's children were old enough to ride, and the cycle began again.

Tony's last four years were comfortable, but lonely. In 1952 when we moved to a different farm, all the horses, except Tony, were sold. Since these horses did not make the move, Tony believed they had remained at the previous farm. Anytime he broke free, Tony ran back to that farm. We knew where to find him, but it was sad watching him search for his companions.

In late August, 1956, Tony contracted sleeping sickness. Dad put him in the barn and made him as comfortable as possible. Tony was twenty-eight years old, and there wasn't anything else that could be done. On his last day, he unlocked the barn door (something he was expert at doing) and made one final effort to find his friends. Dad, who was driving home from Roland, met him about a mile from the farm. Tony's walk was feeble and uncertain, but his stubborn independent spirit drove him forward. With the help of Paul, Dad got him home and put him in the pasture. Within hours Tony was dead.

I arrived home the following day. My summer had been spent lumbering in Idaho. The news of Tony's death saddened me, but I felt no real grief. I had just turned twenty-one, and my childhood years seemed somewhat remote. Also, twenty-one-year-old young men, proud of their newly acquired man hood, do not allow themselves to become emotional over the death of a Shetland pony.

The usual procedure when a farm animal died was for the rendering truck to be called. However, as a child, I had made Tony a promise that he would be buried. For a gravesite, I selected an area of the pasture, which was shaded by a row of elms. The ground was hard, and, as I dug, I could not help being thankful for Tony's small size. After a few minutes, Dad joined me. We said little, each of us satisfied to dig and think his own private thoughts. The grave was soon ready.

With the aid of the tractor, we pulled Tony to the site. There was no way of lowering him into the grave, so Dad and I pushed and the stiffened carcass fell awkwardly into the hole. We quickly began filling in the grave, neither of us wanting to look at the silent, twisted lump that had once been Tony. As I shoveled the dirt, tears began to flow. Inside the twenty-one-year-old man, was still a five-year-old boy. Also, I suddenly realized I was burying more than a pony. I was burying my childhood.

Raygun, ridden by Richard Ullestad

Rocket, Raygun, and Raven

There is a saying about Shetland ponies that goes, "Once you're old enough to control a Shetland, you're too big to ride it!" Anyone who has ever owned one knows the truth of this bromide. The small size of the Shetland, the very thing that attracts the child in the beginning, is what eventually causes him to look with envy at larger and faster horses.

I was satisfied riding Tony until I was nine. Since we had no saddle horses, I turned to my Uncle Les, who then owned a number of colts and fine riding stock. He acquired his small stable by breeding light draft mares to registered American Saddle and Arabian studs. The horses that resulted were spirited, strong, and well proportioned. Two of them turned out to be something special. Oddly enough, the two were dropped the same spring.

Rocket, sired by an American Saddle stallion, was a beautiful sorrel mare. She was a gentle, good tempered animal, who carried herself with mettlesome self confidence. One glance told you she had class. Les worked hard with her and taught her the five American Saddle gaits. She took to the rack, (a fast stylized walk) as if it were as natural as eating grass. In a horse show, her fluid movement from one gait to the next was a delight to watch. After finishing her paces, she would stretch out for the judge, and, with the calm assurance of a winner, wait for her ribbon. Seldom was it any color other than blue. Her competition was not of the quality one would find at a national horse show, but she won over the best that Central Iowa could offer.

An Arabian stud sired the second colt. The foal grew into a massive strawberry roan stallion, who stood over sixteen hands high. His name was Raygun. From the beginning, his Arabian blood was evident. He never seemed to tire. His movements were graceful and effortless. Even when he was standing still, which was seldom, he appeared to be in motion. I don't ever remember Raygun standing with his head dropped. He carried himself with a pride that bordered on haughtiness.

Like Rocket, Raygun was entered in horse shows. However, unlike Rocket, he was not at home in the show ring. Although he won many ribbons, he found the ring confining. He disliked the prancing and posing required of a show horse. Often he lost the blue ribbon by impatiently tossing his head and pawing the ground. Raygun was at his best in the open country where he could move with his natural, long, striding gait. Everyone who saw Raygun agreed he was magnificent. To me, he was much more. He was awesome.

I had hardly learned to control Tony when I began to beg Les to let me ride Rocket and Raygun. Until I was eight, he wisely refused. Then, under careful supervision, I was allowed to ride Rocket around the farmyard. She was as easy to ride as

JERRY L. TWEDT

Tony was difficult. With Tony, you had to be constantly alert for his bag of tricks. He would stop short, try to scrape you off against a fence, go under low tree limbs, dart into open barn doors, or pull one of a half dozen other nefarious schemes. Rocket, on the other hand, was so well trained and well-mannered that she instantly responded to your wishes. The slightest touch of a rein turned her. A gentle tug on the reins stopped her. If you leaned forward slightly and nudged her with your heels, she broke into a rocking chair canter. Rocket was a true pleasure horse.

My ability to handle Rocket gave me confidence and impressed Les, but he still refused to let me ride Raygun. He refused, that is, until a summer evening when I was nine.

Dad, Pete, and I drove to Les' farm at dusk. When we arrived, we discovered that Don and Richard Ullestad, teenage boys from Ames, were already there. These boys were the sons of family friends and had named Rocket and Raygun. Both were excellent riders. Don, the older brother, rode Raygun, while Richard was astride Rocket. We were just in time for a race.

As usual, they were riding bareback. In fact, this was the way all of us rode. Some of my friends had saddles, but they seldom bothered to use them. I didn't own a saddle until I was fourteen. All the riding I describe in this chapter, other than the horse shows, was bareback.

Don and Richard slowly started the horses down Les' quarter mile long lane. Raygun and Rocket knew they were going to race and impatiently pulled at the reins. Raygun went into

84

a side-stepping dance, which he performed when he wanted to race from the road up to the farmyard.

In addition to her show ring abilities, Rocket could run. But, she could not match Raygun's speed. Therefore, to make the race more even, Don took Raygun twenty-five to thirty yards down the road, while Richard started from the end of the lane. This meant that Rocket had a straight quarter of a mile to run. Raygun had to negotiate a ninety degree turn before he could really begin to move.

The semi-darkness kept us from seeing the start of the race. However, in the quiet of the rural twilight, we heard a yell, followed by the beat of hooves. Not being able to see the horses actually made the race more exciting. As the hoof beats grew louder, we all strained our eyes to see who was leading. The darkness would not give them up. Then, when the pounding hooves seemed to be on top of us, Rocket and Raygun burst into view and hurtled toward the finish line! Raygun won by a length.

Don and Richard reined in the horses and rode them back to where we were watching. Both horses found it impossible to stand still. The racing blood was still boiling, and, as their hides glistened with sweat, they tossed their heads, and impatiently pawed the ground.

"Want to race, Pete?" Don asked.

"Sure!" was Pete's reply.

I darted in front of Pete. "Me too! Let me ride Raygun!"

"Ok." Don said, as he jumped down.

Much to my surprise, neither Dad nor Les said a thing. Pete jumped on Rocket and Don helped me up onto Raygun. I gathered in the reins. Don let loose of Raygun's bridle, and I was on my own. I was also in trouble!

Raygun, sensing immediately that I was no expert rider, started for the barn. No one had asked him if he wished to race again. He wanted his oats! Luckily for me, all the barn doors were closed. I turned him back toward the lane, but he was having none of it. He went into his side-stepping dance and paid no more attention to me than he would to an annoying horsefly. I knew everyone was watching, and I was very aware that unless I could get Raygun under control, I would be told to dismount. In desperation, I kicked Raygun with my heels and slapped him with the reins. Much to my amazement, this had the desired effect, and Raygun was soon trotting down the lane after Rocket.

Riding Raygun was as different from riding Rocket as running the rapids is different from canoeing on a placid lake. There was nothing gentle about Raygun. He was all stud! There was a sense of raw, uncontrollable power about him that made a simple jog around the farmyard an adventure. It was only because of many hours of careful training that he even tolerated me.

We reached the end of the lane, and, once again, I had trouble. Raygun didn't want to go the extra thirty yards down the road. He turned in tight circles and refused to leave Rocket.

"Let's race from here," I suggested to Pete, hoping he wouldn't notice how frightened I was.

"No!" Pete shot back. "You wanted to ride him. Get him down to that first telephone pole!"

Pete knew how I was feeling. And, in true, big brotherly fashion, he was enjoying my fear. This made me mad, so I jerked hard on the reins and kicked Raygun with my heels. He responded by half rearing, then danced his way to the starting mark. I had no more than arrived at the designated pole when Pete yelled, "Go!"

Every muscle in Raygun's massive body seemed to explode. He jerked his head forward, which pulled me down over his neck, and lunged ahead. With each stride he gained speed. Les' lane loomed ahead like some angry predatory beast waiting to devour me. I was convinced that Raygun could not make the corner. He was sure to fall! I pulled on the reins with every ounce of strength I could muster. Raygun was surprised and confused. He broke stride momentarily, then angrily took the bit in his teeth and charged forward. From then on, I was strictly along for the ride.

When Raygun reached the lane, I closed my eyes. I truly felt I was going to die. Then, in a moment that is frozen in my memory like a slow motion instant replay, Raygun, with the body control of a ballet dancer and the sure-footedness of a mountain goat, turned the corner and raced up the lane!

With a straight quarter of a mile ahead of him, Raygun lengthened his stride and really began to fly. He homed in on Rocket like an eagle swooping down on a rabbit. The gap between the two horses steadily narrowed. It was as if some force was holding Rocket back, yet, at the same time, catapulting Raygun forward.

I could see Pete hitting Rocket with the reins to urge her on. I did nothing but hang on! I had no interest in who won or lost. I was just praying to survive! Raygun continued to gain on Rocket and was only a length or two behind when we crossed the finish line.

Raygun kept running until we reached the barn, then came to a sliding, bone-jarring halt. I gratefully poured myself onto the sweet, safe, Iowa earth. Don came running up and took the reins from my hand.

"Why did you lose?" He asked disgustedly.

"I...I didn't know," I muttered.

Don took Raygun into the barn, and I walked somewhat unsteadily over to where Dad and Les were standing.

"You did all right, Jerry," Les said.

Dad smiled. "Were you scared?"

"Yea," I said, the relief evident in my voice.

Both men laughed. However, I think they were relieved that I was still in one piece.

I didn't ride Raygun again until I was a teenager. He was a man's horse, and no child had any business even sitting on him. I was lucky nothing happened...very lucky.

The fact that I had ridden Raygun impressed Les, and he asked me if I would like to break some of his yearling colts. I immediately agreed. The thought of being the first to ride a colt appealed to me. In my over active imagination, I saw myself astride a vicious bucking bronco, who would do anything to throw me from his back. Naturally, for every move he made, I made a counter move, which kept me serenely in control. It was a great dream! But, like most flights of fancy, completely lacking in truth.

The similarities between a bronco and a yearling begin and end with the fact that they are both horses. A yearling is still a baby. He is innocent, and usually, quite dumb. He is too dumb to buck. I broke several yearlings, and their response to the first ride was always the same...bewilderment. I would ease onto the colt's back, and he would stand there, too confused to do anything. The difficult thing was not staying on. It was getting the colt to move!

The only danger involved in breaking a yearling was the first time you took him out on the road. I dreaded this part of the training more than any other. The problem was anticipating what the colt would do when he confronted his first speeding car. Usually, he would shake with fear as the car approached, then, as the vehicle roared past, he would jump in the ditch. This is what I expected to happen. What I feared was that the horse would become so panicky, that he would jump in front of the car. My dad told me of a boy who had been killed this way.

With one exception, every colt I broke, jumped into the ditch. The one who didn't was a full sister to Raygun. She had no name. I called her the "Little Arabian". We didn't get around to naming her because she was sold while still a yearling. Like Raygun, she was a strawberry roan, and, although only a colt, she showed the same spirit and speed. However, being a filly, it was obvious she would never match Raygun's size or his overpowering presence.

The first few rides on the little Arabian were uneventful. She was bright and quickly caught onto what was expected of her. My chance to take her out onto the road came one day when two friends rode into Les's yard. I preferred to take a colt out with other horses because they had a calming effect.

Getting the little Arabian to leave the farmyard and go down the lane proved to be a small problem. She didn't want to leave her friends. But, thanks to Tony, I had faced this situation many times, and soon had her out on the road. We hadn't gone two hundred yards when I heard a car approaching us from behind. My heart began to pound and I tightened my grip on the reins. A car coming from the rear was what I dreaded most. At least when one came at you from the front, the horse could see it and somewhat prepare himself. But, coming from the rear, the poor animal was aware of nothing but a monstrous noise.

The little Arabian's ears caught the sound, and I felt her body tense. I edged her toward the ditch, hoping I would not fall when she jumped. When the car was almost about to pass us, the idiot driver decided to honk his horn. The little Arabian's tension turned to panic. Instead of jumping in the ditch, she began to run!

I was scared stiff! What frightened me most was not having any idea what the little Arabian might do. An image of the filly and myself plastered against the windshield of the car flashed through my mind.

The car and the colt sped along side by side. I couldn't understand why the car didn't pass. Then I glanced at the car and saw that the driver was a young teenager, and that he was grinning at me. He thought I was racing him! I violently shook my head, but he kept right on grinning. I began to tug on the reins with all the power I could muster. This had no effect on the little Arabian or on the youthful driver. Not only did he keep grinning, he waved at me!

I will never know what finally made the young man pass me. Perhaps, it was the frightened, pleading look on my face, or, more likely, he became bored with the whole thing. Whatever the reason, he floored the accelerator and sped around me. The resultant cloud of dust had a slowing effect on the colt, and I was able to rein her to a halt. When she stopped, I jumped off the trembling animal. As I waited for my friends to catch up, both the little Arabian and I stood in the hot Iowa sun and shook as if it were thirty below zero.

The worst day I had riding and the closest I came to serious injury occurred one Saturday morning the summer I was breaking the little Arabian. There were six of us racing from our farm to Les's. Loren Jacobsen, whose grandfather lived across the road from us, and I had exchanged horses. He was riding the little Arabian and I was aboard an old Paint, named Dewey. Now, Dewey had been around a long time and knew most of the tricks, while I still had a lot to learn.

The halfway point in the race was the Nelson farm. As we

neared the farm, there wasn't a length's difference between the six horses. I was amazed at how fast Dewey could run. It had the makings of a great race!

As we reached the Nelson lane, Dewey decided he had run far enough and turned in. Dewey and I parted company halfway through the turn. He headed for the barn and I landed on my hands, knees, and head on the gravel lane.

I was stunned at first. Then my knees began to hurt. I was sure I had broken them both. About this time, blood began flowing into my eyes. A rock had opened a small cut in my forehead. The cut didn't amount to much, but it did make me look bad. It also gave me a scare.

I was not the only one who was frightened. Mrs. Nelson and her daughter came running out of the house. They were convinced I was at death's door. Mrs. Nelson wiped the blood from my head and sent her daughter for water and bandages.

"Are you all right, Jerry?" Mrs. Nelson asked anxiously.

I replied with a long, loud moan.

"Where does it hurt?"

"My knees!"

Mrs. Nelson looked startled. We both glanced down at my legs and discovered that my pants were torn, and that both knees were scraped and bleeding.

"Doesn't your head hurt?" Mrs. Nelson asked, as she wiped more blood from my face.

"No."

"Are you sure?"

"Maybe a little bit," I lied. It really didn't hurt! But I

92

realized I couldn't convince her of that. She just didn't understand about my solid granite head.

Her daughter came running with the water and bandages at the same time as my friends rode in. I was the center of attention. Being a natural born ham, and aware that nothing was seriously wrong with me, I played the wounded warrior role to the hilt. I didn't cry, but as Mrs. Nelson cleaned me up and bandaged my head, I gave out suitable moans. When she was finished, Mrs. Nelson asked if I could walk to her car.

"I...I think so," I replied, in what I thought was a tragic, yet courageous voice.

"Ah, he's not hurt!" Pete said. Pete had seen my sick act before.

As I climbed painfully to my feet, my knees really did hurt, I gave my big brother an "Oh, how could you say such a terrible thing" look. Mrs. Nelson did likewise, then gently helped me to the car.

Mother was quite upset when she first saw me. But she soon ascertained that my wounds were superficial. She put iodine on my knees. Then I did cry! She checked the bandage on my head, and told me to rest. There was no sense in continuing my act. Mother also had seen it before.

I turned on the radio and listened to "Let's Pretend," "Armstrong Theatre," and "Grand Central Station". I loved radio drama, and the time passed quickly. I especially liked the opening of "Grand Central Station". With the sound of a powerful steam engine in the background, the announcer explained how the train thundered along its tracks, then dove into the tunnel beneath the Hudson, and emerged at Grand Central Station. It was exciting, and I dreamed of taking that trip myself. Years later, I did arrive in New York by train. But, instead of an overland express, I debarked at Grand Central from a New Haven Line commuter train. No excitement or romance awaited me. Just millions of faceless people.

After the radio shows, Dad came in from the field and we ate dinner. I told him about my fall and proudly added that I had not cried. He cautioned me about riding strange horses and told me to rest that afternoon. I promised that I would.

Resting can be a terrible bore when one is nine years old. So, about two o'clock, I left the house and went to the barn. The little Arabian was in her stall munching on some hay. I really didn't intend to go for a ride...it just sort of happened. As I bridled the filly, I told myself I would ride around the farmyard. But, when I mounted her, I realized I couldn't do that because Mother would see me and demand that I return to the house for more resting. Therefore, I had no choice, but to go out onto the road.

It was a mistake. I had no more than turned out of our lane, when the little Arabian laid back her ears and charged for Les's farm. I was not too surprised. The little filly made a habit of running away with me. She wanted to go home to mother.

Usually, I would let her run herself out, but I was in no mood for a runaway. I jerked hard on the reins, then began sawing the bit in her mouth by pulling one rein, then the other. She angrily fought the bit, but did begin to slow down. As I approached the Nelson farm, I almost had her under control. Then, as we passed the lane where I had fallen a few hours before, the little Arabian jumped in the ditch. She did not throw me, but her momentum drove her into the fence on the opposite side. My foot caught in the woven wire and off I went!

I landed on the seat of my pants, so the only thing hurt was my pride. However, there have been few times in my life when I have felt as mortified as I did at that moment. I took pride in my riding ability, and to fall off in front of the same house twice in one day was too much!

I immediately leaped to my feet because I had visions of Mrs. Nelson and her daughter running out to doctor me again. I glanced at the house, and, thankfully, there was no one home. Having hung onto the reins when I fell, I quickly leaped on the little Arabian's back and headed her for home. It just wasn't my day.

Breaking horses for Les was fun, but it had one definite drawback. Once the colt was trained and fun to ride, Les would sell it or take it back to his farm. Consequently, I asked Dad for a horse of my own. Dad could not afford to buy me one, but he promised me a foal. This arrangement was fine with me.

Bonnie, a small, strawberry roan draft horse, was bred to a beautiful American Saddle stallion. He was black with a white stripe down his face and had four matched white stockings. Just watching him prance around gave me goose bumps. I wanted my colt to be a stallion and look just like him.

While Bonnie carried the unborn foal, I concentrated on coming up with a suitable name. I quickly discarded the popular horse names. I wanted something special! Months went by, yet I could not decide upon a name. None seemed to jump out and demand to be used. I was beginning to worry that the foal would arrive without my having chosen a name, when a cowboy serial came on the radio. I don't remember what the show was called, or the hero's name. But, the hero's horse was a big, black stallion called, Raven. And, as the hero chased the bad guys, he shouted, "Ride 'em, Raven!" Raven! That was it! My horse was going to be a big, black stallion. The name was perfect.

Raven arrived early one morning in the spring of 1945. I was more or less asleep when Dad called up the stairs, "Jerry, Bonnie's had her colt!" Those words had the effect of ice water being thrown on my face. I was up and dressing before Dad could leave the stairwell.

When I reached the small pasture near our house, Bonnie and the foal were invisible because of a heavy ground fog. I called out to Dad, who answered from the far end of the pasture. I quickly climbed the fence and ran toward Dad's voice. Within a few yards, I saw Dad standing a short distance from Bonnie. I didn't see the foal.

"Where's the colt?" I asked Dad when I reached him.

"Not so loud!" Dad ordered in a whisper. "He's behind Bonnie."

"Is it a stallion?"

Dad nodded and smiled.

"Can I go pet him?"

Dad shook his head. "Not yet. Bonnie doesn't like us

being this close."

I was about to edge around in back of Bonnie, when Raven decided it was time to eat. He struggled to his feet and shakily made his way to his breakfast. As he nursed, I was afforded my first real look at him.

My reaction was one of disappointment. Although his mane and tail were black, his hide was sort of a mouse color. Instead of four white stockings, he had three, and in place of a white stripe down his face, he had what resembled a white question mark. He also seemed so small and fragile, not at all the great, black stallion of my imagination.

Dad must have sensed my feelings. He took a long look at Raven and smiled. "Yes sir, he's a good looking colt!"

"Do you really think so? He...he's kinda' wobbly."

"What do you expect?" Dad laughed. "He's only a couple of hours old!"

I felt stupid. I had seen enough foals to know that all newly born colts weave around like drunken sailors. For some reason, I had expected Raven to be different.

"Don't worry, Jerry," Dad said. "He's going to be a good one."

Dad was right. In a few weeks, Raven was prancing around the pasture examining every hole, weed, and tree. He learned to know his small world with a thoroughness that would have been the envy of Sherlock Holmes. I spent hours watching him explore and learn the life around him.

Bonnie, who was by nature nervous and untrusting, didn't especially like having me near. But Raven was curious about this two-legged creature who came to visit, and soon began to enjoy my company. Not that we played much. Every time I tried to run with Raven, Bonnie interfered. She thought I was trying to separate them. I never liked Bonnie, but, I must admit that she was a good mother.

Since Bonnie would not let me approach Raven, I was forced to sit nearby and wait for him to come to me. At first, he advanced stiff-legged, his head outstretched, ready to bolt at the slightest movement. As he began to know me better, he became less cautious. It wasn't long before I was able to pet him and scratch him behind the ears. He liked that. He also liked cookies!

What I remembered best about those early months, was sitting beside Raven while he slept. After we shared my cookies, he would lie down, and, as I scratched his ears, fall asleep. At times, he even put his head in my lap. It did not happen often, but I felt most privileged when it did. I was only ten years old, but I realized these were special moments. I also discovered that little colts snore.

Raven grew into a handsome, large stallion. He stood almost sixteen hands high. His hide turned from mouse color to a lustrous blue roan. I could always count on knowledgeable horsemen to give him an approving nod.

Although powerful and spirited, Raven was by nature gentle. He never kicked or bit, and was genuinely careful when ridden by an inexperienced rider. Unlike Tony, he returned love received with love given. For example, he would not run home if I fell off. When I discovered this, I tested him many times by pretending to fall. I would lie very still on the ground and watch him through half closed eyes. His reaction never varied. He would lower his head and nuzzle me until I jumped to my feet. Even when mares were around, he refused to leave. Raven is the only horse who ever registered any concern for me.

When Raven was a yearling, we moved to a farm two miles outside of Roland. This was, by far, the best farm my dad rented. The house was small, but the land was excellent and the out buildings, all painted white, were beautiful. The huge barn with its gambrel roof was especially magnificent. March 1, 1946, moving day, was gloomy, but the family's spirits were bright. All of us felt this farm held great promise.

We were right. For different, individual reasons, the years spent there were enjoyable for us all. To my younger brother, Paul, and myself, the delight came from our neighbors. Our cousin, David Twedt, lived only three quarters of a mile up the road, and Paul Eide lived directly across the road. The four of us became great friends.

Our first meeting with Paul Eide was not very promising. In fact, it couldn't have gone much worse. However, to appreciate the story, one must first know something about Paul and his parents.

Paul was the only child of Lester and Anna Eide. He was the joy of their lives. Anna fussed over him like a mother hen, and, until we moved across the road, had him tied safely to her apron strings.

It was a warm, spring Saturday when Paul first ventured across the road to our farm. The catalyst that brought him over was the arrival of a group of my friends from Roland, who had ridden out on their bikes. We were in the middle of a wild game of cowboys and Indians when Paul arrived.

"Can I play?" Paul asked, apprehensively.

We stopped the game and gave Paul the once over. All of us immediately saw that he was different. Not only was he younger; he was eight and we were eleven. He looked as if he were dressed to go to town. His shirt was new, his blue jeans were pressed, and his hair was combed! Nobody ever combed his hair unless it was Sunday or a schoolday.

"Sure," I said. "You can play. But you'd better go put on some old clothes."

"These are old clothes," Paul answered.

"They are?" I looked around at the other guys, and we all shrugged. "OK. You can be an Indian."

The rules of our game were simple. The Indians hid and the cowboys searched for and captured them. Of course, the Indians could also capture the cowboys. Paul had little experience being an Indian, and soon found himself captured and tied to a tree. Poor Paul had even less experience being tied to a tree. When his captor threatened to "string him up," he began to cry. Paul was released, and with his hair messed, his shirt wrinkled, his pants dirty, and taunts of "cry baby" ringing in his ears, he ran for home.

Much to my surprise, Paul came back that same afternoon. He had on a fresh shirt, clean and pressed jeans, and once

100

again, his hair was combed, but there was a determined look about him that hadn't been there in the morning. It was my first inkling that within Paul was a reservoir of cold courage. However, Paul's day of trial was not over.

We were in the middle of another chase. Paul, my brother, Paul, and I were being pursued by the guys from town. I took what the army calls "evasive action" and ended up trapped against a high wooden fence and the stock tank. The only means of escape was up and over a corner of the tank. My brother and I had done this before, but Paul had not.

Splash!

Paul went all the way under and came up coughing and spitting. His hair and face were covered with green algae that grows in stock tanks. We pulled him out of the tank, cleaned him off, and did our best to calm him. Nothing worked. He was much too frightened. He charged for home, tears streaming down his face, hair matted with algae, shirt and pants soaked, and his water filled shoes sloshing with every step.

I thought I was in for real trouble. I imagined Anna storming over and railing at my mother for the horrible things done to her son. Much to my relief, the afternoon and evening passed with no phone calls or angry visits. There is no doubt in my mind that Anna was upset. As she scrubbed the green out of Paul's hair, she must have wished we had never entered her son's life.

But, the next afternoon, following church, he was back for more. We had introduced him to the rough and tumble world of boys' play, and nothing or no one was going to keep him

101

from participating.

At the center of our play were the horses. My brother, Paul, who was six, was going through the man-making experience of controlling Tony. David was still riding Beauty. I was in the process of breaking Raven. This left Paul Eide without a horse. Not for long. Within a few weeks, his father bought Paul a beautiful gelding named, Terry. Terry was a light sorrel in color, stood about fourteen hands high, and loved to run. It wasn't long before the four of us were racing up and down the road and across the fields.

Anna was used to having her son playing quietly in the yard, so it is no wonder that seeing him leading the pack in a four horse race bordered on the traumatic. Years later, Anna told me how she used to stand at a window and watch us. She said her heart was in her mouth most of the time. She must have longed for the return of those calm, pre-Twedt days. Yet, she enjoyed having us around. We were her "wild Indians!" And, it was obvious that Paul was having the time of his young life!

Nothing could match the excitement of racing bareback down a country road. There was the feeling of wind rushing through the horse's mane onto your face. There were the smells of grass and corn and earth and sweat. There were the sounds of hooves striking gravel, and leather reins against hide, and the intake and expulsion of powerful equine lungs, and the high pitch urging of unchanged, male voices. Most of all, there was the sensation created by your legs gripping the straining muscles of the magnificent animal beneath you. Your legs became conduits through which your desires and the horse's responses were passed. Because there was no saddle, you were one with the horse. He could feel your excitement. You could feel his desire to win. Each fed on the other. The result was a joyous adrenalin rush for both horse and rider. It was glorious fun!

The fun continued until March of 1949, when we, again, had to move. This was a blow to the entire family. We all had grown to love the farm on which we were living. Once we children learned of the move, we begged Dad to find a farm within the Roland school district. Our greatest dread was changing schools. Dad found just one farm within the district for rent. It was only 120 acres, and the land was relatively poor. But because of our pleas, and against his better judgement, he rented the farm. It proved to be a bad mistake.

Within three years, our financial situation grew desperate. A normal farm debt had ballooned into an intolerable burden. Like so many men who had continued with a general type of farming, Dad had his back against the wall. Luckily, in January of 1952, Dad met Bill Thorsen. Bill had a farm near Ellsworth for rent. This farm specialized in raising hogs and turkeys. Dad became a partner in this venture and, with the aid of Bill, made the transition from farming to agri-business.

In the bleak winter of 1952, the transition was yet to be made. There was no cash, and the family needed many things. Sadly, Dad made the decision that all the horses, except Tony had to be sold. I think Dad was surprised at how calmly I took his pronouncement. I was somewhat surprised myself. However, I was sixteen years old and had developed other interests. I was also well aware of our impossible financial situation, and realized that Dad would not be selling the horses if he had any other alternative. Even though I loved Raven, I was not about to make a scene. Dad already had more problems than he could handle.

On a cold, snowy, day in February, the horse buyer came out. Paul and I were sent to drive the horses from the pasture into the barnyard. In addition to Raven, there was Paul's horse, Trigger, a three year old full brother to Raven; Bonnie, the mother of Raven and Trigger; and a delightful, little suckling filly, sired by Raven.

The horse buyer looked them over and offered Dad seventy-five dollars each for Raven and Trigger, and fifty dollars for Bonnie and the filly. Dad argued, but to no avail. It was a take it or leave it offer. Dad had no choice. A few days later, while Paul and I were at school, the horses were loaded onto a truck and taken away. I never saw Raven again.

In stories and movies, the Black Stallion always wins the race, Big Red prevails, and Lassie comes home. Not so in real life. By my sixteenth year, all of the horses in my life, except Tony, were either sold or dead. Rocket died from eating moldy corn. Raygun was blinded by a pheasant hunter and, eventually, sold to the glue factory. And as for Raven...I would love to think he was purchased by a family who lived on a beautiful farm with a large pasture, but, in all probability, he shared Raygun 's fate. These animals deserved better. They gave countless hours of pleasure and provided memories, which, fifty years later, remain vibrantly alive. I humbly thank them.

❧ **The Three-Holer**

Some are mirrored from ceiling to floor. Many are equipped with Roman tubs, separate showers, bidets, and double sinks. A few are large enough to house a minor league baseball team! I "heard tell" of an old man who had a room so large he kept a small electric cart at the door just to get him to the stool on time!

I am, of course, referring to the modern bathroom. What was once a small, utilitarian space has become a status symbol. Water from gold plated faucets flows into an Italian marble tub. Expensive rugs sit like little oases on a hand painted tile floor. Towels, the size of small sails, lie waiting to wrap the bather in luxurious warmth. And hanging above is a chandelier which would not be out of place in a modest European palace. All this is a far cry from the room's humble ancestor, the three-holer.

Actually, the three-holer was a misnomer. I knew of only one three-holer the entire time I was growing up. That one belonged to my Uncle Mike Jacobson. I will get to it in a moment. Most outdoor toilets, also known as outhouses, had two holes. Usually, one hole was slightly smaller than the

Typical Three-holer.

other. This was known as the "Mama" hole. It is obvious what the larger hole was called.

There was no mistaking which of the farm buildings was the three-holer. It always stood near the house, but off by itself, almost as if the other buildings did not want to associate with it. The dimensions were approximately five feet wide, five feet deep and seven to eight feet high. The roof was peaked and shingled. Almost without exception, the exterior needed a coat of paint. The interior was never painted. And, nine chances out of ten, one of the two door hinges was broken. Why this "necessary" was left in such a state, I do not know. But you could "bet the farm" that the last building painted and the last one repaired was the three-holer.

The interior was, to say the least, spartan. It consisted of a rough wooden floor and an enclosed, sanded, wooden bench into which had been cut two holes. That was it. No mirrors, no towels, and often, no toilet paper. More on that later. There also were no windows, and electricity was as foreign as Chinese food. I am sure this is why a half moon or small circle was cut high above the door. Unfortunately, none of the outhouses I frequented were so equipped. So, going to the bathroom at night was a little spooky, especially if you had an older brother who howled like a wolf and scratched on the door!

I mentioned earlier that my Uncle Mike had a three-holer. Without a doubt, it was the Cadillac of all outhouses. It was built next to a storage section of the house. This portion was connected to the main house by a screened in breezeway. There was even a sidewalk from the house to the three-holer.

Once inside, it was evident that this outhouse was something special. There was a finished quality to it. You felt like you were in an actual room. Great care had been given to its construction. And, not only were there three holes, the holes were beveled! What's more, there were beveled lids that fit neatly over the openings when the bench was not in use. Now, that was class!

When I was young, I always made sure to heed nature's call at least once while visiting Uncle Mike's farm. The attraction was the third hole. This "baby hole" was just the right size for children. It was such a pleasure sitting manfully on that opening without having to fear falling into the lower depths. In the normal two-holer, falling through was a real possibility. I can remember carefully sliding my little bottom over the opening and then bracing myself with my hands on either side of the hole. Relieving one's self under these conditions was awkward and uncomfortable. However, doing so did build character.

Actually, now that I think about it, the three-holer played a major role in building a farm child's character. Courage was necessary to venture out into a moonless night and push open the outhouse door. Often, little furry creatures decided the three-holer was a cozy place to spend the night. Having a raccoon or large rat dash out as you entered was somewhat disconcerting. And it was right down frightening to settle unto the bench and see two bright beady eyes staring up at you.

Self-control and self-discipline also were learned in the three-holer. Self-control was usually a summer course, whereas self-discipline was more a winter subject. During the summer months, numerous species of the insect world took up residence. Most of these were harmless; however, the bumblebee struck fear into the hearts of all human visitors. Great efforts were made to keep this pest as far away as possible. But on occasion, the unmistakable sound of a bumblebee buzzing overhead was heard. Much worse, of course, was to hear the buzzing coming from the lower reaches. Let me tell you, it takes a truckload of self-control to sit still while a bumblebee flies within millimeters of your exposed bottom!

An equal amount of self-discipline was required to frequent a three-holer on a cold winter's day or night. There was no way to heat an outhouse, so if it were ten below outside, it was ten below inside. And, if the wind were howling, the drafts blowing through the walls were capable of powering an America's Cup yacht. Add having to brush snow off the bench, and it is no wonder trips to the three-holer were as few as possible and amazingly brief.

Not so in the summer. Lengthy visits were a wonderful way of avoiding work. They also were often educational and, perhaps surprisingly, enjoyable. Sunlight streaming through cracks illuminated millions of dust particles, which were, otherwise, invisible. These particles were my first introduction into the microscopic world that surrounds us. I delighted in picking out one particle and following it until it floated out of the sunbeam. Depending on my mood, the particle was either struggling desperately to reach some unknown destination or was just taking it easy, enjoying the sunlight and the soft summer air.

Equally fascinating were the spiders. It was great fun and

more than a little humbling to watch them work. They were constantly weaving, yet there was never any meaningless or wasted motion. The results were geometrically perfect and absolutely stunning, especially when a ray of sun bathed the intricate construction, causing it to shimmer as if made of silver threads. Deadly silver threads.

Many times I watched a flying insect entangle itself in the web and frantically struggle to free itself as the spider gleefully danced down its handy work. There was no escape. Death was swift, the feasting leisurely. The drama gave real meaning to the nursery story line. " 'Come into my parlor,' said the spider to the fly." I discovered one can learn a great deal from spiders.

If not watching spiders or dust particles, I usually looked at the catalogue. Now, some young readers not "privy" (I couldn't resist) to the protocol of a three-holer may be wondering why there was a catalogue in an outhouse. The reason was purely practical. As I mentioned earlier, there was often no toilet paper. I can hear the groans. But as unsatisfactory as pages from the catalogues were, they beat the hell out of corn cobs! Yes, cobs actually were used. Now you know the origins of the saying, "Rough as a cob".

What a boy read in the catalogue was an accurate indicator of his age and his fantasies. Small boys were interested in toys. Older ones gravitated to saddles, firearms, and watches. Those who were experiencing strange sensations and racing hormones stared in wide-eyed wonder at pages advertising female underwear.

There is no doubt that the catalogue was a male adolescent's first peek into the strange and alluring world of women. There were ads for dresses, slacks, perfumes, and, most important of all, lingerie. Many fantasies were fueled by those sweet, young things demurely modeling bras, panties, and slips.

In my thirteenth year, there was one model who seemed to look right at me. She was a beautiful brunette with a body that was built for the *SPORTS ILLUSTRATED* swimsuit issue. I fell in love! When I looked at her, I am sure I blushed. If I did not, I should have. Oh, the thoughts! I memorized which page she was on, so I would open the catalogue to the pages just preceding hers. I slowly turned the pages, tingling with excitement. Then, there she was! Gazing just at me with her teasing, brown eyes.

This one-sided love affair continued for nearly two weeks, until, quite literally, we were torn apart. On that fateful day (dramatic background music, please), I discovered, to my horror, that her page had been ripped out! Who could have committed such a heartless act? How could they have done such a thing? It was a sacrilege! I was devastated for almost fifteen minutes.

Actually, the lingerie pages were often the first ones to disappear. I believe this was an attempt by Mother to keep my brothers and me from the sin of lust. The attempt failed. Then again, it could have been my father who tore out the pages. Wise man that he was, he might have realized that without these pages to stir our imaginations, we would spend less time in the three-holer and more time working.

I noticed that females spent as little time as possible in the outhouse. They all hated it. And still do! If you doubt me, just look at the faces of the women who are lined up to use a port-o-let at some large, outdoor function. There isn't a smile to be seen. Teeth are clenched. Lips are pursed. Eyes stare straight ahead. Only necessity keeps them standing in the line.

I have come to believe this revulsion is genetic. I have it on no scientific evidence whatsoever that females have a special gene that programs them to despise the outdoor toilet. My theory is that the gene developed because of brothers. Male siblings, since the construction of the first outhouse, have enjoyed peaking into, rocking, or throwing projectiles at the outhouse when a sister was the occupant. Not that my brothers and I ever did such a thing. The fact that my sister, Herma, has a slight scar high on her lovely forehead from being hit by a tin can is not our fault! She should never have run out the door.

Herma had other reasons for disliking the three-holer. She, more than anyone else in the family, had a knack for finding strange creatures there. The strangest of all was discovered when I was twelve.

My friends and I were playing hide-n-seek on horseback. This was one of our favorite games, as it combined hiding and racing. On this beautiful summer afternoon, I "allowed" my younger brother, Paul, to ride my horse, Raven, while I rode our Shetland pony, Tony. Paul, who was always pestering me to ride Raven, thought I was being a great guy. Actually, I had developed a devilishly clever plan.

When Paul was "it", I quickly rode Tony to the three-holer.

There, I pulled and tugged the reluctant pony into the outhouse and shut the door. Tony was not happy, which was not unusual, when I included him in one of my devilishly clever ideas. The more clever the idea, the less he liked it.

I watched the game through one of the cracks. Very quickly, the other boys were caught or had dashed home free. I laughed as they all began looking for me. It was then that Herma, who was fourteen, approached the three-holer. Seeing the door shut, she sweetly asked, "Is anyone in there?"

"Me!" I answered.

"Oh, it's you," she replied, in her most imperious, big sister voice. "Well, hurry up!"

"I can't."

"Why not?"

"Just 'cause I can't!"

Tony also wanted me to hurry. He showed it by stepping on my toe. "Ouch!" I screamed. Tony did not appreciated loud noises. His nervousness elevated to panic. He began to twist and prance, trying to find the door. I suddenly had a vision of attempting to explain to Dad why the three-holer now had two openings instead of one.

"What are you doing in there?" Herma demanded.

"Nothing!" I answered, almost as panicked as Tony.

"You come out right now!" Herma ordered, and pushed open the door.

Tony saw the opening, reared, twisted, and bolted passed Herma.

My poor sister screamed and ran for the house. Life had not yet prepared her for a pony in the three-holer.

Any writing concerning three-holers would not be complete without at least mentioning Halloween. For reasons, unknown to me, tipping over the outhouses on Halloween was considered great sport. Even better than tipping them over was putting them in strange places. Favorite locations were Main Street, on top of any building on Main Street, on the front lawn of one or both of the parsonages, or best of all, on the stage of the high school assembly hall. It can be safely said that some teenage boys worked harder on Halloween than any other time of the year.

Most everyone who was born in rural America before the 1940's has a favorite Halloween three-holer story. Mine was told by Uncle Leonard Twedt during a noon meal. He laughed so hard tears rolled down his cheeks.

It seems about 1915, there was a grumpy, old farmer, who was disliked by all of his neighbors. Because of his ornery disposition, the man's toilet was a favorite target on Halloween. He let it be known to everyone who would listen that he was fed up. Any boy caught tipping his outhouse would get the business end of a twelve gauge shotgun.

Halloween arrived. So did the boys. The night was moonless, cold, and blustery as the boys crept up the old farmer's lane. Although they pretended not to be afraid, they were. They were especially concerned that the farmer's dog, a large Collie-Shepherd mix, would hear them and wake the farmer.

Soundlessly, they approached the farmyard, eyes searching the darkness, hearts pounding. All was quiet. The dog was either sleeping or out finding his own Halloween fun.

The boys scurried across the farmyard to the three-holer, which was in a direct line to the side door of the house. Carefully, they drug the outhouse about ten feet behind the hole, but still in a direct line to the door. To their satisfaction, the boys saw that the hole was practically invisible. Then, they began making noise, pretending they were having trouble tipping over the three-holer.

"Watch out!"

"Don't let it fall!"

"Push!"

"We're making too much noise!"

Within seconds, the angry farmer, wearing nothing but long underwear and flopping five buckle overshoes, burst out of the side door. True to his word, there was a shotgun in his hands.

The boys let the three-holer drop and raced for a cornfield about thirty yards away. The farmer, loudly swearing in Norwegian, charged after them like an angry bull.

SPLAT!

The farmer never mentioned the incident to a soul. But, within forty-eight hours, most of the county knew about it. Uncle Leonard swore that he was not one of the four boys. However, if you had known my uncle, you would be as skeptical of his disclaimer as I am.

In recent years, the port-o-let has become a common sight at any large, outdoor gathering. If you have frequented one, you may think you know what it was like to use a three-holer.

Wrong. A port-o-let has no cracks, no catalogue, no bees, no character, and no soul. It is a cold, impersonal place. No one would consider staying in one a moment longer than necessary. The three-holer was family. The port-o-let is strangers.

The demise of the three-holer began in the late '40s. The depression was over. World War II was history. Times were good. Farm women demanded and got indoor plumbing. By the '60s, a three-holer still in use was as rare as a draft horse in harness. Both, once indispensable, disappeared with the small, self-contained, family farm.

Farm kitchen of the period. Cook range is from around 1910.

The Kitchen

The farm kitchen was a combination cook house, meeting hall, communications' center, dining room, bathhouse, first-aid station, study hall, dressing room, play area, and, when necessary, juvenile court. It was truly a family room. The reasons for the kitchen's omnibus character were basic: no indoor bathroom, no central heating, and the farm wife's desire to keep the dining room and parlor clean, in case company dropped by. Odd as it may seem, the kitchen served all of these different functions with a minimum of confusion.

Any discussion of a farm kitchen has to begin with the distinctive aroma. I say distinctive because each one smelled slightly different. They all smelled great. Just different.

The foundation of this difference was the fuel burned in the cook range. Corn cobs gave off a rather acrid odor. Coal was pungent and musty. Wood, which was by far the most pleasant, produced an aromatic, sweet scent. Since these fuels were often used in various combinations, the smells from the firebox was in a constant state of flux, as were the cooking odors, which came from the top of the stove and the oven.

Food preparation took hours, so the indescribable aroma of

freshly baked bread would blend with the tangy scent of rhu-
barb pie. And these, in turn, would mingle with the smells of
a simmering pot roast, boiling potatoes, and cooking vegetables
picked fresh from the garden. To this bouquet were added
flower, spices, molasses, honey, soap, and floor wax. All of
these aromas, combined with the perspiration and musk of the
women who produced and conducted them, created each kitch-
en's atmosphere. It was in this atmosphere that the family
lived.

The kitchen was generally a light and cheerful room, and
almost without exception, the middle area was dominated by a
sturdy table covered with a brightly colored oil cloth. It was
here the family ate ninety percent of its meals.

When not in use for meals, the table served almost any
function ranging from workbench to writing desk. And, just as
in the movies, it even at times became an operating table.
However, instead of a hero with a bullet wound, the patient was
usually a newly born pig having trouble breathing.

The cupboards and refrigerator were similar to those found
in any town or city kitchen of the period, but the sink was
something else, again. Due to no indoor plumbing, there were
no faucets. Instead there was a small pump connected to a
cistern. The water from this pump was soft rainwater and good
only for washing clothes, dishes, and dirty little boys. The
drinking water had to be carried in by pail from the deep well
outside. Most drinking pails had a porcelain finish and sat on
a stand beside the sink or on the sink board. If it were a classy
kitchen, the dipper matched the pail.

Another interesting aspect about sinks was their drains. Some drains connected to pipes and emptied themselves into the ground, while others drained into five gallon pails directly below the sink. The problem with the latter system is obvious. Before the farm wife could pour anything down the drain, she had to make sure there was room in the pail. And, when the pail was full, some poor soul had to dump it. I say poor soul because emptying the pail was one of my jobs.

Getting the pail out from beneath the sink was no easy job...especially for an uncoordinated boy like myself. Dad had enclosed the sink with a wooden cabinet, so as to hide the pail. In doing so, he put a one-by-two brace beneath the door. This brace did help keep the cabinet solid, but it was a real obstacle in removing the pail. Instead of being able to slide the pail, I had to lift it over that miserable brace. And since the pail was almost always near overflowing, lifting it out of the cabinet without spilling was nearly impossible. My greatest fear was that I would spill all that dirty water over Mother's clean floor. I never did, but there were few times I did not have puddles to mop up.

The heart of any kitchen was the cook range. It was here that all food was prepared, and all canning and baking done. Standing on its squat iron legs, the old cook range looked indestructible. And to a large extent, it really was. With the exception of the heating gauge on the oven, which never seemed to work anyway, there was hardly anything that could go wrong. My mother's range was used until the day it was sold for junk.

All ranges looked pretty much alike. They measured approximately fifty by twenty-five inches, and stood about thirty inches high. On the back of some ranges, raised above the surface about twenty-four inches, were small compartments used to keep food warm. The front of the stove was often decorated. Our range had a white and tan porcelain finish on the oven door.

As you faced the range, the left hand section was the fire box. Above the fire box were "burners" on which the frying and cooking were done. These burners were circular pieces, which could be removed from the range's surface. By doing so, a farm wife could put a skillet or a pot directly over the flame. Below the fire box was a compartment for ashes.

The center of the range was devoted to the oven. It was large and spacious, and with the exception of a heating element, looked much the same as any modern-day oven. The surface above the oven was not nearly as hot as that above the firebox, so it was here the pots were put to simmer and some special baking was done.

To the right of the oven was the reservoir. It held approximately ten gallons of water and was the only source of hot water in any quantity. However, it was not a very dependable source. When the range was not in use, the water quickly cooled.

Between the ages of seven and twelve, I was responsible for the care and fueling of the range. I took over from my brother, Pete, and served until my younger brother, Paul, relieved me. During those years, I was more or less in charge of keeping the cob basket and coal bucket filled, carrying water for the reservoir, and helping Mother clean out the ashes. I say more or less, because Mother had to catch me before I did anything!

What I liked best about the range was the oven door. Not the oven...the oven door. After being out on a cold, wintry day, there was no better place to thaw out than sitting on the oven door. The heat would penetrate my back and spread through the rest of my freezing body like hot syrup saturating a pancake. If my brothers and sisters also had been out, we fought over who would get to sit on the door first. Since Pete was the biggest, he usually won. This brought great cries of anguish from the rest of us, and such statements as, "You always get to sit on the door first!" and "Just wait 'til I get bigger!" Naturally, Mother was none too thrilled with us sitting on the oven door at all, to say nothing of fighting over who was to sit first. There was always the very real possibility that the door would break. But, she didn't dare yell at us too much because she loved to sit there herself. In fact, Mother was sitting on the oven door the first time she and I had a serious discussion.

It was December of 1941, and I was anxiously awaiting Christmas. Much to my distress, I was told by a fellow first grade classmate that there was no Santa Claus. And, what was worse, only babies believed Santa was real. I certainly didn't want to be considered a baby, so I pretended that I already knew old St. Nick was make-believe. However, the idea of there being no Santa Claus deeply disturbed me, so I asked Mother about it as soon as I got home from school.

"Mom," I blurted out, "is there really a Santa Claus?"

Mother smiled at me from her seat on the oven door and said, "Of course, there is!"

"Are you sure? Gary told me that Santa Claus was pretend."

Perhaps it was the way I asked the question, but for whatever reason, Mother knew it was time to lay to rest a child's most beautiful illusion. She put me on her lap and, as gently as she could, explained to me that Santa was not a real person, but that he represented the joy and spirit of Christmas.

I solemnly listened to her and then asked the question that was really bothering me. "If Santa Claus doesn't bring the presents, who does?"

"Daddy and I do." Mother replied.

"Oh," I said, jumping up. "OK!"

After all, to a six-year-old, it is not who gives the presents that is important, only that they are given!

During the days leading up to Christmas, the cook range performed a very special task in our home. It baked the lefse.

Lefse, a flat, circular, unleavened bread, was a Christmas delicacy at our home. Probably the best way to describe lefse is to compare it to a potato pancake. They look much alike, only lefse is thinner and larger. To my Norwegian ancestors, lefse was a staple food; but in the years following the emigration to the United States, it became holiday fare.

When the time came to make the lefse, usually in early December, Mother prepared the dough and rolled it out into individual lefses, each a circle measuring about sixteen inches in diameter. Then, Dad baked them on top of the oven portion of the range. Getting the lefse from the table to the stove, and flipping them over so they could bake on both sides, was a delicate operation. To accomplish the task, Dad used the small piece of wood that fits in the bottom of a window shade. He carefully eased the stick under the lefse until it was in the center. Then, he gingerly lifted up the stick and carried the lefse to the stove. With a slight flipping motion he laid one half of the lefse on the range. Next, he slowly twisted the stick, causing the top half to roll flat onto the stove top. When it was time to turn the lefse, he repeated the process. Watching Dad bake the lefse was great fun for me. There was drama to it. Would the lefse break, or wouldn't it? Would Dad be able to turn it over without tearing it, or wouldn't he? Dad was very good. He seldom ruined one.

Lefse is still made around Roland, but, since there are no more cook ranges, it is now baked on large circular electric lefse grills. The lefse is baked mostly by older women, and then sold to people who love to eat it but do not have the grill or the "know how" to make their own. Unless some of the younger women learn to make lefse, the traditional Christmas dinner of lutefisk and lefse will become only a delicious memory.

Another gastronomic delight which seems to be fading from the scene is homemade bread. There was no smell more pleasant than the aroma of baking bread. It seemed to permeate the air. Just walking into the kitchen made one's mouth water.

When I was small, Friday was Mother's day for baking bread. It was the one day of the week she didn't have to yell at me to get the coal and cobs. While the oven heated, Mother formed the loaves and buns. What I loved most about this was punching the dough back down after it rose.

How mother knew when the oven was heated to the proper temperature is still a mystery to me. Since the gauge never worked, Mother put her arm into the oven, paused a moment, then either put more fuel into the fire box or popped in the bread. However she did it, the results were delectable!

One of the depressing aspects of farm life during the nineteenth and early twentieth centuries, was the family's isolation from other people. This situation was dramatically altered when telephone poles and miles of line became a common sight along the country roads. Not only did the telephone connect surrounding farms, it also enabled the rural family to communicate easily with the outside world.

The kitchen was the natural place for the telephone to be installed because it was the central gathering place. Installation there made it convenient to answer one's own calls and handy to listen in on the calls of one's neighbors. The fine art of "rubber necking" was born and nurtured on the rural lines of Ma Bell.

A rural party line often included up to fourteen phones. It will come as no shock to learn that the line was generally busy. Having so many on one line was annoying, but sometimes it proved interesting and even hilarious.

We had the old wooden, wall crank-telephone, the type which has become so dear to antique enthusiasts. Phoning someone on an old crank-telephone was not as simple as just dialing a number. If you wanted to call a person who was not on your line, you had to crank one long ring. This would connect you with "Central," to whom you would give the number you wished to call. If you did not know the number, you could always just ask for the person by name. The operator knew everybody in the community.

However, if you wanted to call one of those who shared your party line, it was not necessary to go through Central. All you did was crank the ring that was designated in the phone book for that party. For example, our ring was three long and three short. Another farmer might have one long and two short. A third family might have one long and three short. The reason it was necessary to have individual rings was because when you rang one party on a line, the phones of all who shared that line would ring also. It is no wonder then that it was common for two or three parties to answer the same call.

It also was common for four and five way conversations to develop. Two women would be talking. One would ask a question that the second party could not answer. A third woman, who had been rubber necking, would chime in with the answer. Then, someone else would join, and, before you knew it, half the women on the line were talking to each other. These conversations were fun for the women involved, but pity the person who wished to make a call! Those party line group therapy sessions could last for an hour.

"Rubber necking" was considered bad form, but most everyone did it to some extent. Even during short conversations, it was rare not to hear two or three telltale clicks of the receivers being lifted. This used to annoy me...no, in truth, it made me damn mad! But I never did anything about it until one day I was calling from high school for Mother to come pick me up. She must have been outside the house, because I had to ask Central to ring several times. As I waited, I heard half-a-dozen clicks. By the time Mother answered, I was seething.

"Hello?" Mother said.

"Hello, this is Jerry," I replied. "Wait a minute!"

"What's the matter?"

"I want to make sure everybody is on. Is everyone on?" I asked sarcastically. "I don't want anybody to miss anything!"

There was dead silence on the line.

Can you come pick me up?" I continued.

"Yes," Mother said icily, after a long pause, then hung up.

All the way home from school, I was informed that I was rude, inconsiderate, had a big mouth, and had embarrassed Mother terribly. All of which I am sure was true, but I still chuckle when I think about it.

Although Mother was embarrassed by what I did, the situation was far from being as embarrassing as a party line call that took place when she and Dad were first married. The story was told to me as follows.

The owner of the farm my parents rented was going away for the summer and asked if Mother and Dad would care for his dog. They agreed to take the animal, not knowing she was a huge St. Bernard. Another surprise was her name, Myrtle, which also happened to be my mother's name. My crazy uncles enjoyed this coincidence immensely.

Myrtle, the dog, was friendly enough, but had a habit of

running away every time she was left untied. So, Dad spent more time than he would have liked, chasing around the countryside after Myrtle, Myrtle the dog, that is.

One day at noon, when Dad was in eating dinner, he received a call from my Uncle Leonard Twedt, who, at the time, lived about a mile down the road. The conversation went something like this.

"Hello, Harris? This is Leonard."

"Hello, Leonard. How are you?"

"I'm fine. Say, did you know that Myrtle has run away again?"

"No!"

(At this point, there were audible titters from the rubber neckers.)

"I told you to tie her up with a heavier rope," Leonard continued.

"I did. But she's as strong as a ox!"

(The titters became chuckles.)

"Where is she, Leonard?" Dad added.

"She's down here at my place chasing the chickens!"

(The chuckles became open laughter.)

"Chasing chickens, you say." Dad said.

"Yah, what should I do with her?"

"Well, tie her to a tree, and I'll come down and pick her up."

(The rubber neckers were roaring!)

According to Dad, Mother's face was beet-red with anger

and embarrassment. I doubt, very much, if any of us five children were conceived that night.

Once a week, on Saturday night, the kitchen was transformed into a bathhouse. A galvanized tub was placed in the middle of the floor. The bath water was heated on the cook range in a large fifteen gallon wash-boiler. The boiler was put on the stove and filled in the late afternoon, so that the water would be hot by seven-thirty. Following supper, the kitchen was closed off from the rest of the house, and by bath time, it was almost like a sauna.

The baths began with the youngest member of the family, Linda, and progressed by age, ending with Dad. For the little children, the tub was fine, but the bigger one grew, the more cramped the tub became. Poor Dad couldn't fit in it at all, and was forced to sit on the edge. Being last, Dad faced another problem, a shortage of hot water. Add this situation to the fact that he was forced to wash himself in water already used by six other people, and it is easy to realize why he desired a modern bathroom as much as mother.

It all seems quite archaic when compared to present standards. Today, a house with only one bathroom is thought to be primitive. But, it was all we knew, and no one thought much about it. Considering the time, mess, and work involved, however, I think it is understandable why farm families took full baths only once a week.

Odd as it may seem, I look back on the Saturday night bath with fond memories. This is probably because I remember them from a child's perspective. Whatever the reason, the baths were fun. There was the cozy atmosphere of the kitchen itself, which created a sort of drowsy, warm feeling that gave one a sense of well-being. There also was a great deal of laughter and horseplay as one child got out of the tub and another in. And, when I was older, I had the added thrill of charging through the kitchen when my older sister, Herma, was in the tub. I never saw anything, though. She had the fastest towel in the state!

What I remember best about bath night was listening to the radio. As we had our baths, we would listen to "Truth or Consequences," "Lux Radio Theatre," and the "Iowa Barn Dance Frolic!" The next best thing to going to town and seeing a movie, was listening to "Lux Radio Theatre." I would get so caught up in the story that I would forget to wash. Those were the days when Hollywood was a magical name. When the announcer began the program by saying, "Lux presents Hollywood," I got goose bumps of anticipation. Of all the plays, I still remember, "A Farewell to Arms". At the end, when Henry walked out into the rain, I sat in the tub and cried.

Following "Lux Radio Theatre" was the "Iowa Barn Dance Frolic". It was never as good as the "Grand Ole Opry" from Nashville, but the participants had a lot of fun. The show was broadcast from the KRNT Theatre, Des Moines, and featured the performers from radio station WHO. There was Slim Hayes, Zelda Scott, The Song Fellows, and the program's host, Cliff Carl. For a while, one of the featured acts was the Williams Brothers. Mother remembers Cliff Carl always had to lift the youngest brother, Andy, up on a stool so he could sing into the microphone. It was a warm, happy show, which seemed to be right at home in the steamy kitchen.

The farm kitchen of the 1940's was the most important room in the house, as is its modern day counterpart. Even though the modern farm kitchen is indistinguishable from a suburban kitchen in appearance, it still continues many of the old functions. In it, a farmer and his wife still discuss everything from the price of hogs to which children need what clothing. Ninety percent of their meals are still eaten there. And if a neighbor, relative, or friend drops by, he is still seated at the kitchen table and served a cup of black coffee. In spite of all the rapid, technological changes that have overcome the rest of the farm, the kitchen still maintains its basic character and purpose. It remains much more than just another room...it is home.

Barn in which I first jumped in the hay.

The Barn

T he barn dominated the farm yard much as the Empire State Building once ruled over the New York skyline. Usually painted red and crowned with a gambrel roof, it was the undisputed focus of farm life. Its size and condition were an accurate barometer of a farmer's status. No other building approached its importance, certainly not the house! To the dismay of many a farm wife, the barn made the house look like a casual afterthought.

It was no accident that the barn held center stage. The financial security of the family was, by and large, contained within its walls. One area housed the milk cows; a second was devoted to young calves and feed cattle; a third held the draft horses; and on the second floor was a cavernous haymow which contained the winter feed and bedding for the animals below. No wonder then, that fear of a barn fire ranked equally with such natural disasters as drought, flood, hail, and tornadoes.

In the barn, the farmer began and ended his work day. He had no choice. For, whatever else he did or failed to do, the cows had to be milked twice a day. It made no difference if he had worked until dark in the fields, if it were a holiday, if there were a raging blizzard, if there were a birth in the family, or even if war was declared, those damned cows were always there, waiting to be milked.

Oh, how I hated cows! I was their prisoner. Take the Fourth of July, for instance. Next to Christmas, this was *the* holiday. The family arrived in Story City a little before noon. There we met my uncles, aunts, and cousins and had a family picnic. After stuffing myself with fried chicken, baked beans, potato salad, homemade buns, and at least two pieces of pie, I joined my cousins and other friends riding the tub on the merry-go-round, throwing firecrackers, and doing the hundred-and-one things boys used to do at Fourth of July celebrations. It was a full, fun-filled day. But, even as I played, I periodically looked over at the cow pasture next to the park and was reminded that at five o'clock the fun would end. And sure enough, just when I was enjoying myself the most, Dad would find me and say, "Come on, Jerry. It's time to go do the chores."

My reply was always the same, "Ah, gee! Can't we skip 'em just once?"

My father's answer was always the same, "No".

So with head lowered, fists clenched, and much mumbling, I followed Dad to the car. On the way home, I sulked and mentally wrote my annual "declaration of independence" from cows!

As inconvenient as the evening milking could be at times, it was not nearly as intolerable as the morning milking. Who in his right mind wants to get up at five-thirty in the morning and milk cows? Certainly, I didn't! This was especially true in winter.

A typical morning went as follows.

"Jerry, time to get up," Dad would call from the foot of the stairs. His voice seemed to come out of dense fog, and in my drowsy state, the ninety percent of me that was still asleep quickly convinced the ten percent of me that was awake that I hadn't heard a thing.

Several minutes passed. "Jerry, get up now!" My dad's voice had lost much of the friendliness that had been evident in his first call.

At this point, I would slowly stick my nose out from beneath the stacks of blankets and quilts and take a breath of the sharp air. Since the upstairs was not heated, this breath could quite literally be eye opening! My response, however, was to burrow back under the covers and curl up like a fetus.

"Jerry, are you up?" This question was asked in a stern voice. Dad was losing patience.

"I'm up." I answered in a groggy voice. It was an outright lie, and we both knew it.

I would then peek out from beneath the covers and look out into the darkness and listen to the wind howl and the snow beat against the storm windows. It was all too much! I would throw the blankets back over my head. Nobody could be so heartless as to expect a poor, skinny boy like me to get up on such a morning!

I was wrong.

After climbing two or three steps, Dad would angrily call, "Jerry, are you coming?"

"I'm coming!" I shouted back defiantly.

"Yah, so is Christmas!" was Dad's standard reply.

"I'm up!"

Well, you'd better be! I'm not calling you, again." With that, Dad would return down the steps and go into the kitchen.

There was no hope. I could safely stall no longer. After slowly counting to ten, I would jump out of bed, grab my clothes and shoes, then scurry like a frightened ant down the stairs and into the living room, where I could stand shivering in front of the space heater.

Once I was up, Dad's usual pleasant manner returned. He never yelled at me for making him call so many times. In fact, when the weather was miserable, he often seemed almost apologetic. My father was, and is, a gentle man. It would have required a much harder man than he to scold a sleepy, shivering boy, standing with his bare backside to a space heater.

After I gained control of my trembling body, I began to dress. This was a slow process for two reasons: First, I didn't want to go out and milk; second, each article of clothing had to be warmed on the heater before I put it on.

By the time I was completely dressed, Dad had gone to the barn. This meant I had a few extra minutes to stand in front of the heater. As the warmth from the heater drove away my shivers, a wonderful drowsy feeling came over me. My eyes closed and I slowly turned, like a roast on a spit, so as not to get too hot on one side. All the while I listened to the wind rattling the storm windows. In this euphoric state, the almost irresistible urge to curl up and go to sleep by the heater came over me. It was only the fear of my father's wrath that made me eventually draw myself away from the warmth, put on my coat, overshoes, cap and gloves, and go out into the cold Iowa morning.

I am sure the darkness made the walk from the house to the barn seem worse than it really was, but, even allowing for the psychological factor, the distance covered could be physically brutal. The frigid air took my breath away, and after five or six steps, I was cold to the bone. I felt my nose and cheeks begin to freeze. The wind drove the snow against my face with a force that required me to walk backwards to the barn. As my fingers and toes grew numb, I looked back at the friendly, inviting lights of the house, and I swore to myself I would never own a milk cow.

I never have.

Reaching the barn on such a morning was like finding shelter in a desert sandstorm. Because of the bad weather, the animals were kept in all night, and their body heat caused the barn to be warm and fragrant. There was the smell of manure, of course. But, mixed in with it were the odors of the hay, straw, oats, leather harnesses, and the animals themselves. The sum and total of the smells was most pleasing, especially after the cold air outside. However, my joy in reaching the barn vanished when I saw the cows. They were filthy! No matter how much straw we put down for bedding, the cows always found a way of lying down in their excrement. Each cow had to be cleaned before she could be milked. This was accomplished, none too gently, with an old burlap sack and elbow grease.

Once the cow was clean, I put on the hobbles. The hobbles, two U-shaped pieces of metal, connected by a moveable chain, were mainly to prevent the cow from kicking. They also served an important secondary function. By inserting the end of the tail into the hobble, it prevented the cow from switching the milker in the face...something every cow I milked enjoyed immensely.

Oh, yes! Many people think cows are gentle and sweet tempered. Wrong! They are cunning, calculating, cantankerous critters! Many times I have looked up from milking to see the cow looking back at me. When this happened, I knew I was in trouble. And, sure enough! Every time she either tried to kick me or zap me in the face with her tail! Take my advice...never trust a cow.

We had a beast called "MAD COW". She was a big Holstein, the leader of the herd, mean as sin, and had the fastest tail in Iowa. I hated to milk her worse than any other cow, especially after she had spent all night in the barn. I hobbled her as tightly as I could and made doubly sure her tail was secure before I sat down to milk. When everything was ready, I gingerly lowered myself onto my stool and began to milk, never knowing what to expect. I was very aware of her imprisoned tail and reacted every time she so much as shifted her weight. But, old Mad Cow was a great actress. She stood calm as can be, chewing her cud,, acting as if I weren't even there. And, although I knew better, I would relax and let my mind wander. It was then that she struck! Her urine soaked tail came slashing out from beneath the hobble, and, before I could react, she zapped me across the face. Mad Cow and her tail were important factors in my decision never to be a farmer.

I must admit in all fairness, however, that milking was not all bad. Mostly, yes...but not all. During the summer, I did enjoy going out to the pasture in the early morning to bring in the cows. I would stuff a piece of twine in my pocket, and upon reaching the pasture, would catch one of the horses. I then made a hackamore out of the twine and rode home, driving the cows before me.

I particularly remember one morning when I was nine. The sun had just cleared the eastern horizon, and there was still a crispness to the air. It was one of those mornings when just breathing was pure enjoyment. As I reached the crest of a small hill and looked out over the pasture, I had the strange feeling that I was seeing it for the first time. The dew was heavy, and the reflected sunlight made the pasture look like a shimmering lake of silver. Even the slow moving, muddy creek that wound through the pasture was sparkling. Framing this almost fairyland picture were fields of deep green corn and ripened oats. I took a long, cold drink of water from the pasture's artisan well and looked at this scene for several minutes. I was aware of something special happening to me, but it wasn't until years later that I realized an awareness and appreciation of nature had been born that morning.

Beside bringing in the cows, I also fondly remember the milk wars. These occurred periodically throughout the summer, but only during the evening milking, and only when my brothers and I were doing the milking. Dad did not tolerate milk wars.

The battle usually commenced when my older brother, Pete, was milking the cow directly behind the one I was milking. This gave him a clear shot at my back. And at such close range, he couldn't miss. He pointed one of the cow's port side teats at my back and hit me just above the belt line, causing the milk to run down into my pants. The war was on! I turned sideways and squirted back at him. But, he had his cow for protection, so all I could shoot at were his hands or his legs. All the while, he could rake me from top to bottom. The fight lasted as long as I could stand being squirted or until the cows got so mad at the rough handling that they began to kick.

Quite naturally when our positions were reversed, I wanted to get even and squirt Pete. Since he was five years older and promised to beat me up if I did, I was afraid to act. After each dousing, I racked my brain for a way to even the score. One day, the answer came.

I was sitting on my stool, all wet and sticky and boiling mad, when the idea was born. A lob! Use the same principle as a cannon shooting over a hill. I waited until Pete had moved to a cow three in back of me, calculated the correct angle, then let it fly. My first squirt fell a little short, but the next one was right on the money. Pete's reaction was a surprised yelp!

"Hey! You quit that!" he yelled.

"You started it!" was my reply, as I lobbed squirt after squirt down on his head.

He tried to squirt me, but there were two cows between us so he didn't even come close. All he could do was sit there and take it! Of course, being five years older, he didn't take it very long.

"Jerry, you quit it or I'll knock you in the gutter!" he roared.

"You started it!"

"I don't care! If you don't stop, you're going to get it!"

Not wanting whatever he was in the mood to give, I fired one last squirt, then quit. I had finally gotten Pete wet, and I was one happy boy!

The only good thing I can say about cows is that they had calves. Calves were a lot of fun. I often thought it was a shame that a happy, fun-loving calf had to grow up to be a sour old cow or a grumpy bull.

Dad allowed the calves to suck from their mothers from four to six days before being weaned. Weaning was always a sad time because the calves would cry for their mothers, and the cows would stand outside the barn and bellow for their young. But, if Dad were going to have any cream to sell, he couldn't let the calves drink it all.

Since the calves still needed milk, we gave each a measured amount in a pail. However, before we could do this, we had to teach them how to drink from a pail. This was both maddening and funny.

Dad began by backing a calf into a corner. He then straddled it, one leg on each side of the calf's neck, and pushed its head down into the pail of milk. Usually the poor calf just stood there bug-eyed and blew bubbles. There was always one or two, who struggled, bucked, and ended up knocking the pail out of Dad's hands. I remember one calf who, in attempting to break away, got the handle of the pail caught around its head. It charged around the pen, making gurgling noises and bouncing off the walls and the other calves. I thought the whole thing was hilarious, but Dad, in hot pursuit, failed to see the humor of the situation.

Somehow, the calves learned to drink. It was then they were turned over to me. My problem was just the opposite from Dad's. When they saw me coming with the pails, the calves attacked. To keep from spilling the milk and being knocked over, I did some broken field running that would do a pro half-back proud. My acrobatics didn't always work. More than once, the pails went one way, and I went the other. This situation wasn't nearly as funny as when it happened to Dad.

Even though a farmer spent the majority of his barn time with cows, his favorite area was the horse stalls. There was a quiet majesty about those huge, solid, draft horses that most farmers found hard to resist. A well matched team of pulling horses was a source of pride and envy. Many contented hours were spent grooming and caring for the great beasts.

Until 1942, when Dad bought his first tractor, our barn was overflowing with horses. He had three main work teams, plus two or three brood mares, who could be pressed into service, and a number of colts. When all were in the barn, it was an enthralling place for a little boy. I would sit in a hay bunk and watch as Dad and our hired man harnessed the teams for the day's work. All the straps, buckles, and rings were an endless source of fascination. And when the harnessing was finished,

I begged to ride out to the equipment. Because of the horse's broad back and my short legs, it was like riding a walking barrel. But, I didn't care. I was king of the road!

Like all small farm boys, I was constantly pestering to drive the horses. With two of the three teams, Dick and Dave, and Max and Lady, Dad let me sit in his lap and hold onto the reins, but never when he was driving the third team, Dan and Dude. I never understood why until a late summer morning in June, 1942.

It was nearly noon on one of those hot, Iowa days that makes the corn grow. Our hired man, Orlin Britson, had been cultivating corn with a single row cultivator, pulled by Dan and Dude. I looked down the road from our front porch and saw that Orlin was coming in for dinner. I was about to run down the road and ask if I could drive the horses, when something scared Dan and Dude. In an instant their gentle trot became a dead run! Orlin yelled and pulled on the reins. The horses responded by going faster. As they turned into the farmyard, I could see the whites of their terror-filled eyes. The cultivator careened around the corner, and Orlin either jumped or fell off. He was not hurt, but his face was as white as a salt lick. Dan and Dude ended up in mother's garden. In their wake, they left the cultivator wrapped around a tree, pieces of harness all over the yard, a broken garden fence, and a wide-eyed, seven-year-old boy, who had suddenly gained a healthy respect for the power of a horse.

Approximately a year after that runaway, all the draft horses, except Max and Lady were sold. The tractor had made them superfluous. Some farmers kept draft horses around for sentimental reasons. My Uncle Leonard had horses that went years without feeling a harness. He, like many farmers, was reluctant to sell them because the only place buying pulling horses was the glue factory.

Even so, by 1948, draft horses became a luxury that most Central Iowa farmers could no longer afford. Their stalls were converted to house hogs, cattle, or chickens, and the beautiful harnesses I so admired were left to rot in some forgotten, unused corner. The passing of the draft horse was a true crossroad in agriculture. Thousands of years of cooperation between man and animal abruptly ended. Many older farmers quietly mourned. For them, much of the joy of farming was gone. As for the barn, it was never again the same. There was always something missing. The barn had lost its soul.

The entire second floor of a barn was an open expanse of space. Called the haymow or hayloft, its purpose was to store the winter hay and bedding for the cattle and horses. In fulfilling this function, it also provided a great play area. What could be better than mountain climbing up a twenty foot stack of hay bales, or, with blood chilling yells, attacking a fort made of bales, or playing tag and hide-n-seek on top of, around, and under the bales? Only one thing...jumping in the loose hay!

Until the mid-1940's, when baling became popular, hay was put in the barn loose. Great mounds of hay were loaded onto hayracks and hoisted by rope slings into the haymow. For a few days, before the hay had a chance to settle, it was soft and spongy. These were the jumping days.

One of my earliest memories is jumping in the hay with my older brother and sister. As usual, they didn't want me tagging along. But, I was determined to show them I was big enough to do anything they could. Pete and Herma scampered up the haymow ladder, and I cautiously followed. Since the barn was full of hay, I was required to climb the entire length of the nearly forty foot ladder. Being only five, I hesitated, but my desire to follow Pete and Herma was stronger than my fear, so up I went.

I didn't set any world records going up that ladder, but I did make it. Pete and Herma helped me from the ladder and dumped me into the sweet smelling hay. The aroma alone made the climb worth the effort. Nothing smells better than fresh hay. Naturally, there was much running, pushing, and falling down. But falling was fun! The haymow was like a gigantic featherbed.

Just bouncing in the hay soon became too tame for Pete, so he climbed up to the pulley platform. This was a small platform a the very top of the barn on the rear wall. From there, he grabbed onto the barn rope, which stretched from the large front door to the back wall pulley and down to the ground. He swung himself out, hand over hand, then dropped onto the hay. Since Herma and I were both too small to try it, all we could do was look on with awe and envy as Pete, time after time, repeated his jump. I promised myself that one day I would jump like that. I did, of course, and the experience proved to be everything I had imagined.

As a farm boy grew, the haymow continued to hold attractions. Most every boy had a basketball hoop in the hayloft. On spring evenings, the haymow, emptied of its winter load, would reverberate with the sound of a dribbling basketball. I was never a very good player on a regular basketball court, but in my barn, I was a dead-eye terror! I regularly beat boys who were much better than myself. The reason was that, due to the barn's dimensions, my hoop was set at nine-and-a-half feet instead of the regulation ten feet. Everybody overshot!

Using corn ears to hunt pigeons at night in the haymow was also great fun. First, we broke a number of corn ears in half. Then, we took a flashlight and the corn ears and quietly climbed up into the dark haymow. It was necessary to be quiet so as not to awaken the sleeping pigeons. When a pigeon was spotted and everyone was ready, the boy with the flashlight turned it on. The pigeon froze in the light, and the boys with the corn ears let fly! Although the corn ears made a terrible racket when they hit the barn wall or roof, the pigeon was never in much danger, expecially from me. I had the control of a knuckle-baller throwing into a hurricane. But, the plotting and sneaking around in the blackness of the haymow was the real fun. Nobody actually cared that we never hit the pigeons.

It would be impossible to write about the haymow without a word or two on the delicate subject of sex. Anyone who has heard a farmer's daughter or traveling salesman joke knows that the haymow was the farm's center of sin and lust. Into the haymow a young man would take his sweet, young thing, and, in the mellow darkness, he would make passionate love to her. Ah, if it were only true!

Like so many popular beliefs, the haymow as a rendezvous for young lovers has been highly exaggerated. I'm not saying that it never served that purpose, but anyone knows that a blanket spread in the silent seclusion of a corn field was much safer! There were three drawbacks to using the haymow: one, the farmer might decide to feed his animals at a most inopportune time; two, the hay was scratchy; three, the girl's hair would become entangled with hay, which was a dead give away to any eagle-eyed parent.

Nevertheless, I did listen with great rapture to all the "sex in the haymow" stories. The hormones raced through my body as I imagined myself in the situation. But, alas, imagining was as far as I got. I could never figure out how to con a girl into going up into the haymow with me. The closest I ever came to bodily contact with a girl in the haymow was fouling my sister, Herma, in a basketball game!

The barn was designed to meet the needs of the general family farm. As long as a farmer kept a few horses, a small herd of milk cows, and some feed cattle, the barn remained the center of activity. But, as general farming gave way to specialized farming, the barn went from the status of indispensable to white elephant.

The demise of the once proud barn was almost obscenely swift. It began in the '40s with the selling of the draft horses and was completed in the '50s when the milk cows were sold. Two major areas of the barn ceased to function. If the barn were in good condition, attempts were made to develop these areas for other purposes, but, in most cases the result was less than satisfactory. Farmers quickly learned that they were better off building a modern hog house or cattle shed than trying to renovate the barn. This led to barns being bulldozed or simply allowed to stand empty and rot on their foundations. There is a rueful joke among farmers that in any wind of above twenty miles per hour, anyone with an old barn puts his wind insurance policy in his pocket and pushes against the barn for all he's worth. It is a sad irony that the loss of a building, which fifty years ago would have been considered a disaster, is now thought to be a blessing.

Within another thirty years, the great, Iowa barns will exist only in the memories of old men who spent many happy childhood hours within them. The noble structures will be replaced by squat, characterless, one-story marvels of automated efficiency. Their passing will mark the final mile in the evolutionary journey from farming to agribusiness.

Binder.

Threshing Machine.

The Harvest

For eleven months of the year, it slept beneath the branches of a large, sprawling tree. It was quiet, and despite its monstrous size, ignored. Oh, small boys occasionally crawled up on it and pretended it was everything from an aircraft carrier to a spaceship, but, by and large, it was afforded no thought or consideration. During the winter, huge snow drifts surrounded it. And in the spring, its heavy steel wheels sank into the mud.

But in July, when the grain was heavy on thin yellow straws, a large tractor or a massive steam engine would awaken it from its slumber by pulling it from beneath the shade out into the brilliant Iowa sun. Chains and belts were taken from safe winter quarters and placed upon the conglomeration of drive pulleys and gears. Grease cups were filled and oil was generously squirted on any metal part that moved. Finally, the massive main drive belt, measuring over fifty feet in length and a foot in width, was unrolled and attached to the machine's drive wheel. After a twist was put into the belt, the other end was placed on the flywheel of the tractor or steam engine. The power source was then backed up until the belt was off the

154

ground and taut. Slowly the flywheel began to rotate. With an almost painful groan, the giant machine's moving parts broke the bonds of nearly a year's neglect. Wheels turned. Shakers shook. Gears ground. Faster and faster the flywheel turned, until the monster was in full cry, its jagged metal teeth lashing out to lacerate the imaginary grain. It was threshing time.

For the next month, all attention was focused on the threshing machine as it prowled the countryside, devouring bundles of grain into its bowels. This prairie dinosaur frightened the horses, petrified small children, worried wives and mothers, and fascinated young boys, and, like the dinosaur, is now extinct.

Threshing was the final act of a three-act production. The first act was sowing the grain, which in our case was oats. Very little wheat was grown in Central Iowa.

The sowing process began with preparing the ground. On a typical one hundred and sixty acre farm, thirty to forty acres of the previous year's corn ground was set aside for oats. As soon as the land thawed, usually in late March or early April, this section was disked lengthwise and crosswise. This was done to grind up the old cornstalks and provide a receptive field for the grain. Once the crop had been sown, the field was again disked lengthwise, so that a light layer of earth covered the seed oats.

When it came time for the actual sowing, "the seeder" device, which worked on the same principle as a modern day rotary lawn fertilizer spreader, was attached to the back of a wagon. The top of the seeder consisted of a large hopper into which the seed was dumped. This hopper funneled down into two small adjustable openings. Beneath these openings were two rotary spreaders, which sent the grain shooting out behind and to the sides of the wagon in a twenty foot pattern. The spreaders were powered by a series of small gears attached to to a drive shaft that extended out behind the wagon's right rear wheel. On the end of the drive shaft was a sprocket, which was connected by a flat chain to a large sprocket fastened to the wooden spokes of the wagon wheel. Thus, when the wheel turned, the seeder functioned.

My first experience with sowing oats came on a cold, heavily overcast day when I was five. Rather than keep my older brother, Pete, home from school, Dad decided I was old enough to drive the horses. Mother bundled me up in long underwear and an old red snowsuit, and I proudly stood by my father in the wagon as he drove the team out to the field. It was a big day, for I was not pretending to help, but actually fulfilling a necessary function. Although I could barely see over the top of the wagon box, I felt very grown up.

Once in the field, Dad filled the hopper with oats, put the seeder in gear, and nodded for me to start the horses. "Giddy Yup!" I shouted, with as much authority as my five years allowed, and slapped the reins.

Obediently, Dick and Dave, the old gray geldings I was driving, began plodding the field. The wheels squeaked, the wagon box groaned, and with a hissing sound, the seeder strewed out the grain.

My job was to keep the horses going in a straight line while

Dad concentrated on filling the hopper and making sure everything worked properly. Now, it may not sound like much to drive in a straight line, but if you are five years old and in a forty acre field with no row markings, it can be a little difficult. Dad pointed out things such as fence posts and bushes to guide me, but he still spent half of his time pulling on one rein or the other in order to keep the wagon in line. He kept telling me what a great job I was doing, but I am sure he would have said that even if I had driven in a big circle!

As minutes turned into hours, some of the thrill of doing real work began to lessen. The colder my hands and feet became, and the more often I wiped my runny nose on my sleeve, the more convinced I became that pretend work had certain advantages over the real thing. Had I become cold doing pretend work, I could have quit, run in the house, and warmed myself by sitting on the oven door of the cook range. Real work, on the other hand, forced me to stay put and shiver. I tried to make old Dick and Dave go a little faster, but they were not about to hurry for the likes of me. More and more I found myself looking over at the area remaining to be seeded. And for the first time did something that I was to do in similar situations hundreds of times...wonder if we were ever going to finish!

"Getting cold?" Dad asked.

"A little bit," I answered, not wanting to let him know how cold I was.

"We'll be done soon," he smiled.

And sure enough, before long we had finished our last round and were on the way home.

"You did real fine today, Jerry," Dad said as he patted my shoulder.

These words of praise and the knowledge that Dick and Dave would have us home in minutes made me forget my discomfort.

I bragged to my brother and sister when they came home from school. In fact, I am sure I was a royal pain in the fanny. But, in truth, I was much wiser that evening that I had been in the morning. I had learned the difference between work and play.

Once a farmer had disked in the oats, the crop was out of his hands. If the weather cooperated, his field would be a carpet of green shoots by the first week in May. As the days grew longer and the sun warmer, the shoots grew to stand hip high to a grown man. Then, nature performed her annual miracle. The tall blade-like shoots burst into clusters of grain. Hot, humid days quickly caused the individual kernels to grow plump and firm. As June made way for July, the crop matured and its color turned from a deep lush green to a glowing, golden yellow. Often many of the shoots were unable to hold their burden of grain, and whole sections of the field collapsed. It was time for the second act...cutting the oats.

Unlike the modern self-propelled combine, which cuts and threshes grain in one continuous and efficient process, a threshing machine required a farmer to cut the grain, gather the grain into bundles, set the bundles up into shocks, load the shocks onto hay racks, and then unload the grain into the threshing machine. The time differential between the two systems was enormous. For example, if a farmer had forty acres of grain, a modern combine could easily cut and thresh the crop in two days. Whereas, when threshing, three weeks could pass between cutting and putting the oats into the bin.

The implement used to cut and bundle the grain was called a "binder". It was a direct descendent of the McCormick reaper and one of the most ungainly contraptions ever invented. It always reminded me of an unsuccessful turn-of-the-century airplane created by a mad inventor. This was in large part due to the wooden reel, which folded the grain onto the binder after being cut by the sickle bar.

Excluding the reel, which looked much like the reel on a modern day combine, the left part of the binder was a low metal platform measuring eight to ten feet in length and about four feet in width. At either end of the platform was a roller measuring between five and six inches in diameter. Over these rollers and through tracks, both above and below the platform, was stretched a long canvas. Wooden laths were riveted to the canvas at approximately two foot intervals. The inside roller rotated when the binder moved, which in turn caused the canvas to revolve, forming a conveyor belt on which the grain was carried to the right side of the machine.

The right side of the binder looked like an inverted "V". This was because a large, steel bull wheel, which powered all of the gears, chains, pulleys and rollers, was located beneath the "V". As the grain left the canvas platform, it was drawn to the top of the inverted "V" between two similar but smaller canvases, one placed almost directly on top of the other. The oats were then dumped onto an angled, metal table. When a sufficient amount of grain had accumulated, the knotting arms turned, making a tight bundle bound by twine, and at the same time, kicked the bundle into the carrier below. The bundles collected in the carrier until it was full. Then the bundles were released in a pile by the man riding the binder. He always attempted to drop the bundles in rows, so that shocking was made easier.

The purpose of shocking was to let the grain dry and to keep it off the ground. To achieve this, the bundles were stacked, grain up, six to eight to a shock. Often one bundle, called a cap, was put on top the shock to protect the grain from wind and rain.

My first harvesting job, that of water boy and lunch bearer, was given to me when I was seven. Dad hitched Tony to the cart, and I, with a gallon jar of cold water sitting between my feet, drove from shocker to shocker dispensing the cool liquid. The thirsty, sweat-soaked men always greeted me with the widest of smiles, although, the smiles narrowed a bit when my erratic driving caused the cart to knock over one of their newly set shocks. I was especially welcome at mid-morning and mid-afternoon. Those were the times that Mother sent out coffee and cookies. There was never any danger of the coffee not making it to the men, but as for the cookies...that was something else again. Mother sternly admonished me not to eat any of the cookies. I could have my cookies at home. But, it was usually a long way to the field, and everyone knows you should never travel on an empty stomach. Anyway, that excuse made a lot of sense to me. By the time I was halfway to the field, I found myself searching the cookie bag to see if, by chance, there were any smallish or broken ones. Strangely enough, there always were! Stranger still, even with my pilfering, there were more than enough cookies for the men. You don't suppose Mother actually thought I might take one? Never!

Following three years of being chief water boy, I was promoted to driving the tractor for the binder. This made me an integral part of the harvesting operation. Unlike being water boy, driving the tractor required continuous concentration and fast reflexes. Not only was the driver responsible for maintaining a full cut of grain, but he also had to be alert for mechanical malfunctions and possible obstructions in the path of the binder.

Since the binder Dad and Uncle Leslie Twedt owned jointly was old, most all of the problems that could happen did happen. Rocks knocked teeth out of the sickle bar; chains broke; rivets worked loose, causing laths to break away from the canvases; the wooden reel caught on the metal frame, sending shattered wood in every direction; and most frequent of all, the knotter refused to knot. Any of these problems triggered a great yell of "whoa" from the man on the binder, in my case, Uncle Les. The "whoa" was a carry-over from the days when horses furnished the power.

On days when the old binder decided to be contrary, driving the tractor was an unpleasant and tension filled experience. It also was less than fun for the man on the binder. Uncle Les, who was basically a happy-go-lucky, free spirit, became more infuriated with each mishap. And the more upset he became, the more nervous I became. All of which led to mistakes.

The worst mistake I could make was not stopping when Les yelled, "whoa". Failing to stop would turn a minor breakdown into a major one. But, not stopping was also the easiest mistake to make since it was almost impossible to hear Les yell over the roar of the tractor and the clanking of the binder. Inevitably, when things were going badly, he would have to yell three or four times before I would stop.

"What's the matter with you?" He would say angrily.

"I didn't hear you," I would mumble.

"Well, pay attention!"

When we were back running, I was almost rigid with tension. My foot hovered over the clutch like an angry housewife about to stomp a cockroach. At times, the strain became so great, I would imagine hearing my uncle yell when he did not. Down would go my left foot on the clutch! Down would go my right foot on the brakes! And since he was not prepared for a stop, up would fly Uncle Les out of the binder seat, desperately snatching for control levers to keep from being thrown off the machine.

"What the hell are you doing?" was his usual outburst. I had no trouble hearing this, nor did anyone else within a radius of half a mile.

"I...I thought you said, whoa," I would lamely reply.

Les would shake his head, settle back in his seat, give me his "you are hopeless" look, and motion for me to start up again.

By this time, I was really uptight. To keep from making a false stop, I would look back at Les every time I imagined I heard something. If he had not yelled and I was lucky, he would be studying something on the binder and would not see my questioning glance. However, if my luck was running the way the binder was functioning, he would be staring right at me, shaking his head, and giving me his "you're hearing things again, Jerry" glare. After a few of these scowls, hot anger would compound my tension. I would think to myself, "What right does he have to give me those condescending looks? If he thinks driving this tractor is so easy, let him come up here and drive the damned thing!" Then I would decide not to look back again, no matter what! We would go along until...

"Whoa!"

Did I hear something? Did Less yell for me to stop? Maybe it was my imagination again.

"Whoa! !"

There! I thought I heard something again! Should I look? Maybe something is wrong. Then again...

"Whoa! ! !"

I am sure there were times when my Uncle Les was convinced I was the dumbest kid whoever put on a pair of pants.

When I was eleven, harvesting became more fun. Uncle Leonard joined his two brothers, Les and Dad, for the oats cutting. This provided two binders instead of one. Leonard's son David, who was my best friend, drove for him, while I drove for Les. One of the things that made the cutting more fun was the unspoken competition between the two rigs. From the standpoint of Les and myself, the contest was hopeless. Leonard had a beautiful, new, red and yellow, ten foot binder, pulled by an "M" Farmall, whereas Les and I made do with an old, eight foot binder pulled by a Montgomery Ward Avery.

As we began the cutting, David and Leonard started first with Les and me right behind. I did my best to keep as close to them as possible, but the age of our binder forced us farther and farther behind. After a number of rounds and several breakdowns, David and Leonard would have completely lapped us, and the big red "M" would be about to run us over. David was then forced to slow the "M" to match our speed until we came to the end of the cutting area, at which time I would pull out and let him pass. This was galling to both Les and me, but we always did it. Always, that is, except once.

What was to be known thereafter as the great Twedt binder race began just before dinner on Leonard's farm. Les and I had experienced a rotten morning and had been passed a number of times. On the last round before stopping for dinner (lunch to city people), David and Leonard caught us again. We were at the far end of the field, which was shaped like a large rectangle. Les and I had just started cutting on the short side when David had to throttle down to keep from crashing into us. Les yelled at me. I was about to stop when I noticed he was giving me the speed up sign. My response of opening the throttle was immediately matched by David doing the same. Les signaled for more speed. Again, our increase was matched. Both David and Leonard were laughing. Les's jaw was set. Without being signaled, I gave the Avery more gas. A puff of blue-black smoke from the "M's" exhaust told me David was keeping pace.

As we approached the end of the cutting, I gave Less a questioning look. Should I pull out and let David and Leonard pass or make the turn? Les grinned and motioned for me to make the turn.

The race was on!

I made the turn without slowing down, which almost threw Les off the binder. But David did the same, and the nose of the "M" was only a few feet from the back of our binder. Les gave me the speed up signal. I pulled the throttle wide open.

The old binder rattled and shook, but continued to make perfect bundles. I am sure it had never been worked that hard before, and I know I had never before driven a tractor that fast under working conditions. My excitement became tinged with fear.

I looked back at Les expecting him to tell me to slow down, but instead he gave me another speed up signal! I was in second gear with the throttle wide open, so the only way of getting more speed was to shift into third. I did not even know if the little Avery would pull the binder in third! And there was David only a few feet behind. I swallowed hard and shifted.

The Avery paused for a fraction of a second then leaped forward with a roar. I think the Avery was tired of being passed, too! When I knew the motor would not die, I eased back on the throttle, but we were still going frighteningly fast. I shot a glance back at Les and saw that he had a death grip on the control levers. But, he made no sign to slow down. Perhaps that was because he was afraid of letting loose of the levers!

My shifting to a higher gear caught David by surprise and

the maneuver put some distance between us. Not for long. He too shifted and was soon right on our tail. Both binders were spitting out bundles in an almost continuous stream. The knotting arms kicked the bundles out so hard they flew over the carrier. The shockers, Dad, brother Pete and Olaf Highland, stared in open mouth amazement. I am convinced that no two binders ever cut grain at a faster pace.

The sounds of protest from that old binder were not to be believed. I expected every gear and roller to fly off in a different direction. But, somehow it too was in the spirit of the race and worked like a precision watch. In the vernacular of the '90s, it said, "In your face," to the red and yellow binder!

Before I knew it, we were at the end of the cutting. I slowed enough to make the corner, then turned, thinking the race might continue. But it was time to eat, and Les yelled for me to stop. I shut off the tractor and looked back at Les. He just sat there for a moment, then shook his head and laughed. By any measure of probability, the binder should have been spread over half the field, but there it was, stopped and in one piece. We had defied the fates and won! However, we never tempted them by trying it a second time.

I drove for the binder until I was fourteen, at which time my younger brother, Paul, took over, and I joined Dad shocking. Like so many things, shocking looked easy until you tried it for yourself. I quickly discovered that timing and coordination were necessary if the shock was not going to immediately collapse into a pile of bundles.

If one shocked for any length of time, three items were essential: a good pair of leather gloves, some type of hat, and a long sleeve shirt worn outside the pants. The long sleeves were to protect the arms from being scratched, and the shirt was worn outside the pants to keep out the chaff. It was also a good idea to wear heavy high top shoes because of the sharp oat stubble.

The usual way to shock was to grab a bundle by the twine with the left hand and bring it up under the right arm so that it could be cradled in the right hand. Next, you picked up a second bundle with the left hand, gave it a little toss, and caught it so that it was cradled under the left arm. Then the arms swung forward until they were parallel with the ground, putting the bundles into a vertical position. As the bundles were lowered to the ground, the hands firmly pushed the grain ends of the bundles together so they leaned against each other. You then repeated the process with two more bundles, making sure that those two leaned into the first pair. This was probably the trickiest part of shocking. It was very easy to knock down the original two bundles. Once four bundles were in place, you leaned two more against the original two. You could then add as many pairs as you wished, but we usually put up six and capped the shock with a seventh.

Shocking was not heavy work, but it did require a tremendous amount of bending and even more sweating. The worst time of all was following the heavy noon meal. There were times between the hours of one and three when I was convinced old Joshua had returned and was holding up his rod to stop the sun. The only relief was a long rejuvenating drink of water, which if there were no water boy, came once a round.

A jug of water was put under a shock to shade it from the sun. The shocker was required to work all the way around the field before he could get a drink. I seldom made it. By the time I was halfway, I was so thirsty I could hardly swallow. All I was able to think about was that life preserving liquid beckoning like some Lorelei from beneath the water shock. As the sweat dripped off my face, I tried to tell myself that I could make it all the way around. But when I came directly opposite the water, I usually surrendered and crossed through the uncut grain for a drink. This proved to the other shockers that I was not tough, and was not yet a man. Since I was guilty on both counts, I saw no reason to die of thirst to prove otherwise.

There was a pleasant time to shock. It was after supper when the sun was a soft, red ball in the sky, and the evening breeze was beginning to stir. Because of milking and other chores, we seldom shocked then, but when all the cutting was done, and we wanted to finish the work, everyone returned to the field. It was a congenial time, filled with laughter, stories, and more often than not, a little horse play. The bundles seemed light and almost shocked themselves. In no time, or so it seemed, the task was done. A satisfied silence would fall over all as we looked over the completed field. It was a brief moment of beauty. There are a few sights in this world as tranquil and picturesque as a shocked field of grain bathed in the glow of an orange twilight sky.

Once the cutting and shocking were done, the threshing

machine was pulled from its winter quarters, and the final act of the harvest began. A threshing run (why it was called a "run" is a question I cannot answer) usually consisted of between ten and fifteen farms. According to my father, a rule of thumb was to have ten men hauling bundles, two manning the oats wagon, and one managing the machine. If the run were too small, the operation was inefficient due to the lack of manpower. But, if the run were too large, weeks could go by before a farmer's grain was safely in the bin.

Generally, each farmer owned a share of the threshing machine; however, one man was selected to operate it. He was the only man on the run who did not have to furnish either a hay rack or an oats wagon. He was also the acknowledged leader and arbiter of disputes. To small boys, being in charge of the threshing machine was one of the life's ultimate achievements, and rare was the farm boy who did not picture himself at some future date in this lofty position.

On our run, Uncle Leonard was the man. My most vivid mental picture of Leonard is one of him standing on top of the threshing machine, much like a captain on the bridge of a ship. His felt hat, which he wore winter or summer, is cocked so that it almost touches his left ear; his knees are flexed to absorb some of the machine's vibrations; in one hand is a long-stem oil can and in the other a roll of belt paste; and on his face is an intense expression of concentration as he looks and listens for the first sign of trouble. To me, he personifies the threshing boss.

A threshing machine in operation was an impressive sight.

Most were roughly twenty feet long, six feet wide, twelve feet high, and made of thin sheet metal. Some of the older models were smaller and had wooden sides. On the front of the machine was a hinged feeder, onto which the bundles were unloaded. In this feeder, measuring about six feet long and a yard wide, was a conveyer system composed of wooden cross pieces attached to two flat link chains. Projecting from the cross pieces were nail-like points of steel, which assisted in keeping the bundles moving into the machine. A board divided the feeder lengthwise, permitting unloading from either side.

As the bundles entered the machine, they were attacked by a row of cleaver-like blades. The bundles were torn apart, and the straw and oats fell into the heart of the machine, which consisted of series of shaking screens. Here the oats were detached from the straw and channeled into the oats well. From the well, the grain was augured up to the top of the machine where it was funneled into the long cylindrical spout which augured it out into the wagon. The straw was dumped into a blower cave and then blown by a large exhaust fan out of the cave, through a long telescoping spout onto a pile or into a barn.

Next to the knives at the mouth of the machine, the blower cave was the most dangerous part of the threshing machine. Naturally, this made it of special interest to small boys. Since the fan-shaped hatch which opened into the cave had a latch on the outside, it made a great dungeon when the machine was not in use. Lying in the semi-darkness of the blower cave (my feet braced against the small rim that divided the cave from the large fan) was eerie and a little frightening. I often thought of Pinocchio being swallowed by the whale.

During the noon break, older boys used to love daring a younger boy to crawl into the blower cave. They called him "chicken," "scaredy cat," and "baby," until the boy agreed to do it. Then the conversation went something like this:

"You...you won't lock the door?"

"Nahhh, we wouldn't do that."

"You're sure?"

"Sure we're sure! We wouldn't think of locking it, would we fellows?"

"No!"

"Well...Ok, but just for a little bit."

Once the boy had slid into the cave, the hatch was slammed shut. Immediately, the boy began to yell. The older boys laughed and started yelling things like, "It's threshing time!" or "Start the tractor up, Joe!" Hearing this, the boy panicked and began to cry and pound on the hatch. If the older boys were extra mean, they might even push the starter button the tractor. After a proper amount of pleading, the boy was let out and admonished, under fear of death, not to tell any adult. But, he usually talked, and the affair earned the older boys some time stacking straw or threats from their fathers to "kick their hind ends up between their shoulder blades!"

The job everyone hated on a threshing run was stacking straw. To do the job properly, there was no way of avoiding the chaff and the stinging pieces of straw from the spout. As in shocking, it was necessary to wear a long sleeve shirt outside of the pants. It was also a good idea to keep the collar button fastened, the collar turned up, and wear goggles. No matter what precautions a man took, there was no way to keep from getting filthy dirty.

The worst part of stacking straw, however, was not the dust and chaff; it was the lack of moisture in the mouth and throat. After only minutes on the stack, your mouth felt like it was filled with cotton balls. It became almost impossible to swallow. Many methods of conserving the mouth's moisture were tried. The favorite means was chewing tobacco. My dad, when he was about seventeen, decided to see how the tobacco worked. He took a big chew in his mouth, climbed up onto the stack, and began to work. He chewed and he spat. He spat and he chewed. And, you know what? It worked. He did not have a dry mouth that entire afternoon. Of course, he did not stack any straw either. After ten minutes of chewing and spitting, he turned green and spent the rest of the day lying under the shade of a tree.

Until around 1940, the power source for the threshing machine was the steam engine. According to old timers, much of the romance went out of threshing with the demise of the steamer. I came along too late to have actually worked with one, but I remember, as a small boy, how awed I was by the pressure gauges, fire box, whistle, and the great, rear, steel wheels. Large tractors, usually an "M" Farmall, "A" John Deere, "Oliver," or "Minneapolis-Moline," took the place of the steamer. Although not as colorful, the tractor was more maneuverable, much more dependable, and given enough gasoline, would run all day with little attention. Some old farmers look back on the steamer with a good deal of nostalgia, but at the time of the changeover, there were few who mourned its passing.

No matter what the power source, or how big the threshing machine, neither was of much use until the grain was brought in from the field. For this we used the common, ordinary hayrack. As any modern farmer knows, the hayrack is no longer common or ordinary, but in the 1940's no farm was complete without one. For those not acquainted with hayracks, imagine a flatbed trailer about sixteen feet long and ten feet wide, with a floor of one by twelve's spread about an inch apart. Add to this three feet high frames on all four sides. The frames were constructed of one by sixes bolted to the vertical two by sixes, which in turn fit into slots attached to the bed of the rack. Think of a wooden fence like you see around horse farms built onto the bed. The four sides of the hayrack made up what farmers called "the basket". A ladder, three feet wide and nearly seven feet tall was added dead center in the front of the basket. The ladder made it possible to climb up onto the load when the farmer was finished. Many hayracks also had the back of the basket built up to a height of seven or eight feet. When fully loaded, this rather odd looking vehicle carried an amazing number of bundles.

Loading bundles was an exacting craft, bordering on an art form. Many an improperly loaded rack arrived at the threshing machine minus half of its original contents. To load bundles, you first filled the basket, then began stacking bundles, straw end out in rows along the two long sides of the rack. In effect, you were building two retaining walls of bundles. You erected one side, then the other, then tossed bundles into the middle. By following this procedure, and if properly executed, the top of the load would be about fifteen feet high. Since a solid load of bundles was generally the creation of one man working without the aid of anyone up on the load, a strong back, a certain feeling for proportion, and a good three-tine pitchfork were essential.

I officially joined the threshing run when I was twelve. My job was to drive the horses while my brother, Pete, loaded bundles. The team of horses was old and wise. I was neither. What I was, was excited! I wanted Jim and Lady to be the best team on the run. They had no such aim. Each had pulled countless loads of bundles and in no way shared my excitement. They responded to my commands at an exasperatingly slow gait. No matter how I yelled or threatened, they moved along at their chosen rate, showing complete contempt for my driving ability. When I complained to Dad, he laughed and said that neither one was capable of going faster than a slow trot. A few days later, I was to find out differently.

Pete and I were finishing a field on the Johnny Johnson farm. It was nearly dinner time, and we lacked only a few bundles of having a load. I was in my usual place, standing near the top of the ladder and leaning against the top board. There suddenly was the crunching sound of nails breaking free of wood, and before I knew what had happened, I found myself sprawled on the top of the wagon tongue between the two horses. To say Jim and Lady were frightened would rank among the great understatements of all time. In a moment, their fear transformed them from tired, spiritless draft horses into racing stock!

Down the field we went as fast as they could run. Although I was busy hanging on, I did notice that bundles were flying every which way. Poor Pete! He saw his carefully stacked load disintegrate before his eyes.

I had fallen squarely onto the wagon tongue and, although shaken up a little, was not hurt. As the horses ran, I wrapped my legs and one arm around the tongue and grabbed unto the back of Lady's harness with my free hand. I knew if I fell from the tongue, I would be stepped on by Jim and probably run over by the rack.

The danger of the situation was not my chief concern. In fact, things happened so quickly that I was not really frightened. But I was worried about losing the entire top half of the load. Being stepped on did not bother me. Being yelled at by Pete for losing his load, did! My first thought was to grab the reins. They were within reach, but snatching at them would have meant letting loose of either the tongue or the harness, and I was not about to do either. The only thing I could think of was to try and calm the horses by talking to them.

"Whoa, Jim...Whoa, Lady," I said in what I hoped was a reassuring voice. "Easy now...take it easy...whoa there."

Whether it was my voice or the simple fact that they had run farther in thirty seconds than they had in the previous fifteen years, the team slowed and came to a halt. I crawled out from behind the horses and looked at the load. It was a mess.

The bundles, which had not fallen off, would have to be pulled off and restacked. I thought for sure I was in for a royal chewing out from Pete. About that time, Pete came running. But instead of being angry, he looked scared to death.

"Are you ok?" He panted.

"Yah, I think so."

"What happened?"

"I don't know. I was just standing on the ladder and then fell onto the tongue."

We both looked up at the ladder and saw that the top board was missing. It was only then that I realized what had happened.

"You're sure you're ok?" Pete asked again. "Do you think you can drive?"

"Sure, I'm ok." I said, more than a little surprised by Pete's mother hen anxiety. Pete and I had a very normal big brother, little brother relationship, with all of the fights, arguments, and tears that that relationship entails. But I also secretly believed he was the greatest big brother in the world. So, his obvious concern meant something special to me.

That evening when we arrived home, I told Dad about my fall and how fast Jim and Lady had run. He, like Pete, realized what might have happened. I was sent off to bed while he worked long into the night tearing apart the old ladder and replacing it with a new one on which the cross pieces were bolted to the uprights.

As a boy grew older, there was a natural progression from

driver, to spike pitcher, to having a rack of his own. The intermediate step of spike pitcher was an apprenticeship in learning how to load bundles properly. The "spiker" would help a farmer load his rack, then, when finished, move on to another rack which was just beginning to load. Spiking was actually harder work than having one's own rack because there were no rest periods while waiting to unload. The spiker also had a problem keeping up with the older man. Most spikers were in their early teens, which made it very difficult to match the stamina and strength of the rack owner. Many men, myself included, live with back problems due to attempting to load too fast and pitch too high.

Before a young man was considered worthy of having his own rack, he first had to prove he was mature enough to unload into the threshing machine. There was no escaping the fact that this was dangerous work, and a threshing boss had to have faith that the boy was capable of pulling up to the machine and balancing on top of a load before he was allowed even close to the machine. My time came, quite by accident, when I was sixteen.

I was standing by our old Regular Farmall tractor, which had replaced Jim and Lady in pulling the rack, when the rack up at the machine finished unloading and pulled out. Dad's rack was up next, so I began looking around for him. He was nowhere in sight. The threshing boss (we had moved to a different farm and he was not my Uncle Leonard) motioned for me to pull up to the machine. It was a hot day and I had been sweating freely, but at that moment I really began to sweat.

The threshing boss motioned again. Still no sign of Dad.

I knew I could not just stand there. All the other farmers waiting in line were looking at me. They realized it was my time for testing. I took as much time as possible cranking the Regular into life, hoping that Dad would arrive. He did not.

Guiding a big hayrack loaded with bundles to within a few inches of a threshing machine feeder was no easy task. Perhaps because of beginner's luck, I pulled the rack snugly up to the machine. This gave me a great shot of confidence because I had seen others hit the threshing machine or come in so far away, they had to pull out and make another pass. I crawled off the tractor and, once again, looked for Dad. He was not around.

My throat was dry, and my heart was pounding as I climbed the ladder. I had helped Dad unload before, but only after he had topped the load and there was little danger of falling. Standing by myself on top of a full load, fifteen feet high, was a whole different ball game! The hungry mouth of the threshing machine had never looked so menacing. I had heard stories of men falling into the feeder, but for the first time, saw how easily it could happen.

The threshing boss yelled at me, and I began to slowly and carefully pitch bundles into the feeder. There are few times in my life when I have concentrated as hard as I did then. Before long, however, the load was half gone, and Dad was climbing into the rack to help me finish. He did not say anything, but a broad grin on his face told me I had done well. A few days later, when we threshed at our farm, Dad took care of the oats wagon, and I was given my own rack.

With the exception of stacking straw, minding the oats wagon was the dirtiest job on the run. The oats spout on the threshing machine did not telescope. This meant a great deal of hand scooping was required to keep the oats from flowing out of the wagon. This was especially true when the wagon was nearly full. Many times my father yelled at me for letting the oats overflow. Add the heavy back work to the noise, the chaff, and the oats in your shoes, and it became obvious why taking care of an oats wagon was less than loved.

But it was for this grain the farmers had worked since spring, so the oats were carefully scooped or elevated into bins where they were stored for feed. Few farmers in our area sold their crop outright. If the yield was good, it was a happy farmer, who, after the run had moved to the next job, could look at his large straw stack and bulging bins and know that his animals had feed and bedding for the long winter ahead.

Whenever old threshers get together, one topic is sure to be talked about with a great deal of eye rolling and lip smacking...the food! I am sure I have never eaten as much or as well as on a threshing run. It was like having Sunday dinner everyday of the week.

There was nothing fancy about the meals. But, hungry men who had been pitching bundles for five or six hours had no need and less desire for fancy food. A typical noon meal consisted of a menu such as this: boiled or mashed potatoes; a vegetable or two, usually sweet potatoes, green beans, scalloped corn or creamed peas; some sort of salad, often home grown leaf lettuce with a sugar and vinegar dressing; meat, generally pot roast, pork chops, ham or chicken; homemade bread; and all topped off with freshly baked pie. What a feast! Supper was less extravagant. There was potato salad, cold cuts or meatballs, a salad, a vegetable, bread, and fruit for dessert. It was still a hearty meal, but nothing to match the dinner.

To prepare such sumptuous meals required a Herculean effort on the part of the farm wife. Even so, it was impossible to do it alone. When her turn came to feed the threshers, she would call in a half dozen of her relatives and neighbors to help prepare the food. In return, she would go to their farms to assist them. This was not only necessary, but also made the hard work more enjoyable.

On threshing morning, Mother was up and baking by four o'clock. By five-thirty, when Dad called me, that indescribable aroma of baking bread had infiltrated every room of the house. Mother stopped her baking long enough to get us breakfast, then she and my sister, Herma, started on the pies. Around eight, the other women arrived with extra place settings and serving bowls. After a little socializing, it was time to peel the potatoes, wash the lettuce, shell the peas, and do the hundred and one things necessary for a successful meal. By eleven o'clock, the women were running in three directions at once. Eleven-thirty found the kitchen in complete chaos! But, by twelve noon, the tables were set, the meat was done and everything was ready. What makes it all the more remarkable was that the meal was prepared on an old-fashioned cook range, with the temperature outside ninety degrees in the shade.

Promptly at noon, the threshing machine was turned off, and the men, with their stomachs growling in anticipation, trooped toward the house. Since no woman would allow fifteen to twenty filthy men to wash in her house, wash basins were set up beside a galvanized washtub of water in the back yard. The men also preferred washing outside because they could splash and slop around as much as they wanted. Never has cleaning up for a meal been so enjoyable.

I first removed my shirt, then lathered myself from the waist up. To rinse, I cupped my hands and splashed on water, taking a perverse delight in being as messy as possible. When I was finished, I dumped any remaining dirty water out and re-filled the basin with more cool clean water. I put my face only a few inches from the basin and, again with cupped hands, drenched my face, neck, and shoulders. The cool water ran down my back and chest producing brief moments of sensual delight.

No farmhouse in our part of the state had enough table space to seat twenty men, so two shifts were necessary. Whether you ate first--which was by far preferable because while the second group ate, you could lie under a tree and rest--or second, depended largely on whether your rack was full or empty. A man with an empty rack was always in the first group to eat. This was so he could quickly return to the field for another load. What every bundle hauler strove for was to pull into the yard, see two or three loaded racks in front of him, and then have the threshing boss shut down the machine for dinner. Not only could he take as much time as he wanted to eat, he could have a good snooze afterwards! However, no matter when you ate, the food was guaranteed to be delicious.

A threshing table, if the run were going well and the weather was holding, was alive with boisterous, good spirits. There was much laughing and talking and teasing of the women, who were kept busy rushing from the dining room to the kitchen, filling empty bowls and platters. Often, to the delight of the boys and consternation of their fathers, the conversations were filled with stories of past runs. Even though somewhat embarrassing at times, the stories were good fun. They also provided the boys an opportunity to see their fathers as human beings, rather than just as parents.

Oddly enough, the dinner that stands out in my memory was not due to the food or the conversation, but to the drink. I had just turned sixteen that summer. I stood about six-foot-one and, perhaps, weighed one-hundred-forty pounds if I wore a heavy, winter coat. On that particular, hot, July day, we were threshing at the farm of an elderly couple. We had all been seated for dinner, and the woman of the house was pouring the liquid refreshment. The boys were all getting milk, and the men were asked if they wanted coffee or ice tea. I fully expected a glass of milk, but when she got to me, she asked, "Ice tea or coffee?" I am sure she thought I was retarded by the way my mouth dropped open. All I could think of was that she had asked me what I wanted. She thought of me as a man instead of a boy! The woman asked me again, and, since I couldn't stand coffee and had never tasted ice tea, I mumbled, "Ice tea". I looked at the amber liquid flowing into my glass and began to wonder what I had done. I reasoned, anything that looks that good must taste good, so I took a small sip. It was delicious! I then proceeded to drink three glasses, and would have had more had Dad not begun to give me funny looks. I walked out of that room ten feet tall!

Because of the great quantities of food consumed at a threshing dinner, it was necessary to rest for a few minutes following the meal. The men would lie down on the grass in the backyard or lean up against a shade tree and smoke. The boys, on the other hand, would roll around on the grass as if they were about to die of overeating. However, within a few minutes, one boy would steal another boy's hat, or a game of tag would be started, or someone would take a basin of water left over from washing up and dump it on an unsuspecting victim. No matter how it started, the boys always ended up running, shouting, laughing, and in a mass wrestling match. It was not unusual for a boy to be hungry again before the afternoon's work had begun.

By one o'clock, the men and boys were back at work. The women, after eating their dinner, were relaxing over a cup of coffee and praying that the threshing would be over by mid-afternoon. If that happened, they only had to prepare a lunch, rather than a warm meal. The lunch usually consisted of coffee, lemonade, and cookies or cake. One such lunch, in 1942, will always be remembered by my mother.

Some of the men had moved on to the next farm to start

loading, but most were still at our place when the tractor was turned off and the threshing machine was prepared for the road. The men came up to the yard for lunch, leaving the horses untethered. No one gave this a second thought as the main object in life for most draft horses was to move as few muscles as possible.

My younger brother, Paul, was almost two years old, and my sister, Herma, and I had been assigned to watch him while Mother and the women served the men. As any child will tell you, watching a younger brother or sister is a dreadful bore. It wasn't long before Herma and I were playing, and Paul was nowhere to be seen. We didn't even miss him until one of the farmers pointed to the front gate and said, "Look at that!"

Everyone turned to see Dick and Dave, my dad's team of horses, plodding toward us. Behind, dressed only in a diaper and rubber pants, was brother, Paul. He held the reins in his hands and was running to keep up with the horses. As he reached the yard gate, he pulled on the right rein, and obediently the two horses, who each weighed well in excess of one thousand pounds, turned toward the fence.

"Whoa!" Paul shouted.

The horses stopped and Paul stood there grinning from ear to ear. Mother was standing on the front porch during all of this, a look of shocked horror on her face. While the men cheered and clapped for Paul, Mother darted off the porch. Never before or since have I seen her move so fast. She scooped Paul up in her arms and carried him into the house.

I would just as soon not say what happened to Herma and me after the threshers had gone.

The worst part of the threshing was doing the chores when we got home after a day's work. No matter how tired Dad and I were, we still had to slop the hogs, feed the chickens, pick the eggs, and milk the cows. Many a time, I put my head against the warm flank of a cow and dozed while my hands stripped her of her milk. Once finished, I took a sponge bath in the kitchen sink (we had no indoor plumbing) and fell into bed. No sleep-inducing pills were necessary after a full day on a threshing run.

In 1952, Dad and Uncle Les pooled their money and bought a combine. That was the end of threshing for me. At the time, there were a few small runs still struggling along, but by the mid-1950's, the threshing run had become a part of Americana.

For most farms, the day the combine arrived was considered a happy day. The farmer could harvest grain when he wished and did not have to wait his turn to thresh. The combine was far more efficient, requiring two or three days to do the work that formerly took two or three weeks. To the farm wife, it meant feeding two men rather than fifteen to twenty men. In short, it was a step forward...progress. But, progress always exacts a cost. Threshing forced people to be interdependent. The farmers and their wives had to work together, help each other, and share problems. There was no escaping the need for joint effort. What resulted was a sense of community...people who knew and cared for each other. It is sad that much of this sense of community has also become a part of American History.

Bergen Lutheran Church.

∽ **The Church**

Chairs. Not big chairs. Little, red folding chairs with black padded seats. These chairs are what comes to mind when I think of my early religious training. I was between three and four years old when I began going to Sunday School. These little chairs, made for little people, were what greeted me. I thought the chairs were the greatest idea since God created ponies. I cried when I was told I could not take one home.

In the '40s, attending Sunday School and church was mandatory, not only for my family, but for the vast percentage of the 650 inhabitants of Roland, Iowa, and the surrounding farm community. No matter what else might be planned for the day, church came first. At eleven o'clock on Sunday morning, when the bells of Salem and Bergen Lutheran churches sounded, the town folks and farmers were expected to be at one church or the other. I grew up thinking everyone in the world attended church on Sunday morning.

Since the only two churches in town were Lutheran, anyone of a different denominations or faith had a problem. He could become a Lutheran or drive all the way to Nevada or Ames where there were Catholic churches and other Protestant congregations. Few, if any, made the drive.

It is no accident that the two churches were, and still are, the most impressive buildings in town. The Norwegians who emigrated to central Iowa were simple, deeply religious people, who believed that God's house should be a "proper place". They often constructed their churches before they had decent homes for themselves.

Salem Congregation was formed in 1868 and Bergen in 1874. Salem's current building was constructed in 1915. It is a red brick church with Gothic stained glass windows and two castle-type turrets. Bergen's structure was built in 1929. It, too, is of red brick, but is "L-shaped" and has stone facing on the front.

Why two Norwegian Lutheran churches in such a small community? The answer lies in a theological argument that raged among the Norwegian immigrants during the mid-nineteenth century. It was basically a "high church"-"low church" controversy.

The parent church of both Salem and Bergen was St. Petri, which was located in Story City. The people who formed Salem broke away from St. Petri to have a simpler service, more prayer meetings, and no clerical vestments. Six years after Salem was formed, a second group of people left St. Petri to organize Bergen. This was a friendly break and happened only because the people involved lived closer to Roland than to Story City.

Bergen and Salem are located one block apart, but a state

of cold war existed between the two for nearly one hundred years. As a child, I remember people from Salem, who refused to set foot into Bergen because the minister wore a simple black choir robe. Bergen was too "Catholic"! The bitter feelings died slowly, but they, at last, were laid to rest with the pioneers who hallow the Roland Cemetery. Now, there is a competitive spirit between the two congregations, but no enmity.

The two churches were the social as well as the spiritual centers for the community. Not to be a member of one of the two churches meant almost complete ostracism from what little social life Roland offered. The Luther League for young people met every other week; the men's brotherhood held monthly meetings; and the Ladies' Aid and women's circles met monthly.

Of all the groups, only the circles met in people's homes. Each Circle consisted of twenty to thirty women, who took turns being hostesses. I never attended any of the meetings, but I was under foot on several occasions when Mother or one of my aunts was serving. I enjoyed them because of the delicious cakes which were served and because of the quilting that was done. It was fascinating to watch the women sewing in the various patches and watching a design emerge. It always baffled me as to how so many women could work at one time on one quilt, and still have everything match. At the annual church supper and auction, I looked at these beautifully made quilts and secretly hoped Dad would bid on one. I knew he wouldn't, for they were much too expensive for us.

The big social event of the year was the church supper and auction. At Bergen, where we were members, these suppers were held in the upstairs Parish Hall. The large kitchen off the hall was busy all day with women preparing the food and making gallons of black coffee in huge three-gallon coffee pots. In the Parish Hall, men, usually under the sharp supervision of their wives, set up tables and folding chairs and put on the paper tablecloths. When their work was completed, two hundred people could eat at one time.

Serving began about five o'clock, and by five-thirty, the Parish Hall was full. Since we lived on a farm and had to milk cows and do the evening chores, we never arrived at the church before six-thirty. By then, the line stretched from the Parish Hall, down the stairs, through the lower hall, and back to the church parlor. It was not unusual to see a hundred people waiting in line. A good turnout meant between six and seven hundred people were served.

One of the great tortures of my life was having to wait in those interminable lines. When I arrived at church, I was starving; then, to have to stand in line for nearly forty-five minutes was agony. I could hear the clanking of dishes and the laughter and voices of those eating. The sound of the continual, droning conversation made me angry. I would say to myself, "Why don't they shut up and eat!" And to make matters worse, the delicious aroma of the food drifted down the steps, causing one hundred stomachs to rumble like a symphony of kettle drums.

Ah, but the food was worth the wait. Lefse and lutefisk often headed the menu; and if you were a true son of Norway, the alternate choices weren't important. Some years, ham, fried chicken, mashed potatoes, gravy, cranberries, and scalloped corn were provided. No matter what the main course, there were always an array of homemade pies and cakes for dessert.

The food was served family-style, and one could eat as much as desired. Since almost everyone ate like they would never see another meal, the serving women were in constant motion. Perspiration beaded on their brows as they scurried between the kitchen and the tables. Although their efforts were valiant, the large bowls and platters seemed to be continually empty. The food was not fancy, but it was prepared with loving care and tasted delicious!

When the last growling stomach had been stilled, and everyone had the uncomfortable, yet, pleasant feeling of having eaten too much, the tables were cleared and the auction began. Not everyone stayed for the auction, but enough remained to pack the Parish Hall. The items up for sale, most made by the church women, ranged from quilts to rag rugs and intricately made dresses to simple aprons.

The auctioneer was C.O. Highland. He was a puckish, somewhat bemused individual, who viewed the happenings of Roland with a rather jaundiced eye. He had a sharp mind, a fast tongue, and was an exceptional auctioneer. As with all good auctioneers, Mr. Highland could turn an auction into drama. He knew when to crack a joke, when to scold, and how to make an item seem indispensable. During an auction, he was the star, and he made the most of it.

To add fun to the proceedings, Mr. Highland sold certain

small items to people whether they bid on them or not. These articles never cost more than a dollar or two, so the "buyer" laughed and paid the price. My father was one of Mr. Highland's favorite targets. At one auction, when my sister, Linda, was about one year old, the item was a beautiful pinafore. Mr. Highland took one look at it and said, "Harris, this will look great on that pretty little girl of yours! Sold to Harris Twedt for a dollar and a quarter!" C.O. was right. My sister, Linda, was absolutely beautiful in the dress.

The auction went on for nearly two hours, so we, children, usually wandered off to amuse ourselves elsewhere. When the weather was good, we played tag or hide-and-seek out on the church's spacious lawn. If it were impossible to be outside, we attempted to play the same games inside. As long as we didn't disturb the auction, run too fast, or yell too loudly, we were allowed to have our fun. The church parlor took quite a beating on these occasions.

When we were feeling particularly brave, we ventured into the church sanctuary. Only the altar area was lit, which caused the remainder of the sanctuary to be enveloped in a soft darkness. The farther back we went, the darker it became. Afraid that someone might catch us, we tiptoed to the back of the church, went up the stairs, and sat in the balcony.

I found it very impressive and a little frightening to sit in the darkened church. Bergen's high peaked roof, long rectangular sanctuary, and Gothic stained glass windows produced a cathedral quality. Hanging over the altar and adding to the solemnness, was a huge painting of Christ rising from the dead.

With Christ in the picture is an angel sitting on a rock and cowering Roman soldier. I do not know how good the picture is from an artistic standpoint, but I do know it had a sobering effect on little boys. No matter where in the church one sat, Christ seemed to be looking at you.

This, however, did not mean we always behaved. I think we were all of the mind that believed Christ could not see us if we ducked behind the pews! I well remember one Sunday when I was five. For whatever reason (the devil made me do it) I could not sit still. It was a beautiful spring day, and the last place I wanted to be was in church listening to words I did not understand.

As the sermon began, I was sitting next to my sister, Herma. But, after kicking her "accidentally on purpose", I was swiftly moved between my parents. There I squirmed, hummed, and generally made a nuisance of myself. All of this embarrassed and upset my parents. Dad gave me "the look," which meant I was pushing my luck. But at that moment, I accidentally (cross my heart) knocked the church bulletin to the floor. I quickly jumped down to retrieve it and so discovered a new world! It was a fascinating world of shoes. There were big shoes, small shoes, high heeled shoes, toeless shoes, two-toned shoes, and even shoes with no feet in them. One woman had removed hers. This world below the pew was much more interesting than the one above, so I began to explore. However, before I could discover anything of earth shaking value, Dad grabbed me and, none too gently, sat me back on the pew. He leaned down and whispered, "If you do that again, you'll get a spanking."

Well! This was a challenge. After all, I was exploring. I had discovered a new world. It was my duty to go where no boy had gone before!

So, after a few minutes, carefully watching Dad as I went, I slithered down beneath the pew. I had not even reached the floor when two large hands picked me up and sat me down hard on the pew. Dad was grim.

"Just wait until we get home!" he said, in a whisper that was heard by everyone in the church.

I realized I was in deep trouble, so I did what any enterprising five-year-old would do. I snuggled close to my mother and sniffled.

The service ended and we quickly went to our car. Now, you must understand that my dad loved to "visit". After church was prime visiting time. To go directly to the car was practically unheard of. No question about it. I was in for it.

"Am I still going to get spanked?" I wailed from the back seat of our black 1935 Ford.

"Yes." Came the stern reply from the front.

Desperate measures were required. There was only one hope left. I stood up, put my arms around Dad's neck, and cried all the way home. My last hope failed. Much to my father's credit, he took me upstairs, bared my little bottom, and gave me several good swats on the fanny. I learned a valuable lesson that day. I learned that even if Christ cannot see behind the pews, fathers can.

Although the Parish Hall was used for all big gatherings, such as church suppers, its major function was to house the Sunday School. Every Sunday morning, at ten o'clock, from September through May, the Sunday School gathered as a body for a short song and prayer service. Following the service, the classes separated for the study of the Bible and Luther's Catechism. We were taught by the women of the church. They did their best to pass on their faith and impart theological concepts they, themselves, did not understand.

My class was not overly popular with the teaching staff. In fact, a number of teachers decided to retire after a year with us! None of them considered us bad; we were, as one teacher put it..."trying". The reason for our less than exemplary behavior was boredom. As in so many churches of the period, Sunday School was something to be endured rather than enjoyed. The essential "Good News" of the Christian faith was drowned in a sea of memory work and tedious lessons.

One yearly event in Sunday School, however, was great fun. It was the Christmas program. We began practice following Thanksgiving, and worked hard each Sunday afternoon until the performance. It was our chance to dress up in old bathrobes and pretend we were Wise Men from the East or Shepherds. All the girls wanted to be Mary. Mary was always dressed in a long blue dress and had a white shawl on her head. She sat by a cradle and looked lovingly at a doll in a makeshift manger. While the role of Mary was actively sought by the girls, the part of Joseph was hated by the boys. There were three very good reasons. First, he would be teased about being married to

196

Mary. Second, he had to stand still behind Mary for much of the program. And third, he had to look pious. It was tough enough for any boy to stand still for that long, but to look pious? Forget it!

The stars of the program were the little three and four-year-olds. They usually sang one song, gloriously off key, and recited a simple one-line "piece". No one ever could predict what they would do, and, of course, this is what made them so delightful. Some would cry. Others would wave at their parents. Most would say their piece in tiny small voices. A few would shout the lines. And, there generally was one who proudly announced to the entire congregation that he had to go to the bathroom.

Following the program, each child was treated to a large red apple and a box of animal crackers. The atmosphere was electric. Every child knew that when the Sunday School program was over, Christmas was only hours away. To this day, I think of Christmas when I see a box of animal crackers.

We attended Sunday School through the eighth grade. Then, in preparation for becoming full members of the congregation, we spent the freshman year of high school studying Luther's Catechism. This was called "Reading for the Minister". It should have been called, "Memorizing for the Minister!" Each Saturday morning at ten o'clock, the class met and recited an assigned portion of the catechism. This pre-supposed, of course, that the lesson had been memorized. In my home, going unprepared was a major sin, so Mother kept careful

watch over my progress...or lack of it. Friday night was basketball night, but I couldn't leave the house until I had recited
my lesson to her. This exercise was painful for both of us and
usually ended with her saying, "I'll let you go this time, but
you'll have to study in the morning!" Even with the morning
study, I always required a good deal of help from the pastor.

Bergen's minister was a tall, Lincolnesque man, named
Allen Nelson. He was reserved, yet genuinely warm and
friendly. There was a scholarly air about him. In fact, he had
taught at Luther College, Decorah, Iowa, and I think he missed
the academic atmosphere. His love of teaching became obvious
during our Saturday meetings. Although he was annoyed with
our lack of preparation, he loved questions and enjoyed ex-
plaining Lutheran theology.

While I made no pretense of liking all the memory work,
I did enjoy those Saturday sessions. Mostly for the wrong reasons, I'm afraid. Because of them I was able to get out of a
morning's work at home plus being able to drive the car into
town. Driving to Roland was my big event of the week. Wheel-
ing our Frazier Manhattan over the gravel roads made me feel
like I had, indeed, become an adult. I was only fourteen, and,
instead of having a driver's license, I had what was called a
school permit. This allowed me to drive directly to and from
school. Dad stretched it to include to and from church. I
stretched it to include to and from anywhere in Roland and
participating in an occasional drag race.

The culmination of our Saturday morning efforts came on
a Sunday morning in late May, at which time we were given our

first communion and confirmed as full members of the congregation. Before we could be confirmed, however, we had to be publicly tested on our knowledge of Luther's Catechism. This much feared gruelling was called "catechization" and took place the Thursday evening before Confirmation Sunday. The entire congregation was invited, but, thankfully, only family and relatives came.

The days before my catechization were spent in the seemingly hopeless task of memorizing all the lessons I should have learned during the year's study. As Thursday approached, I found myself fervently wishing old Martin Luther had never left the Roman Catholic Church.

Thursday evening arrived. Along with the rest of my panic stricken classmates, I marched up the center aisle of Bergen Lutheran Church. My parents gave me reassuring smiles, but I could see they were nervous. Having a child do poorly at catechization was highly embarrassing. I took my place and prayed that I would get at least one question right.

Reverend Nelson cleared his throat and explained to the congregation that there would be four rounds of questioning. This meant that each of us would have to answer four questions. As the first round began, I stood stiffly at attention. My throat was dry, my mind was blank, and I felt very warm in my very first new suit.

The first three rounds went quickly, and much to my surprise, I had answered my three questions correctly and without assistance from Pastor Nelson. As the fourth round began, perspiration began running down my neck. I wondered why the janitor had turned on the heat. I tried to concentrate on the questions being asked my classmates, but instead found my mind drifting in a curious fashion. I looked up at the rows of amber colored hanging lamps and wondered how it would be to swing from one to the other, Tarzan-style. I glanced at the clock, and to my amazement, the hands were going round and round. The people sitting near me began to murmur. The heat was becoming unbearable. I wiped my face and became aware that everyone in the congregation was staring at me. I did not know what was happening, but I realized if I didn't sit down, I would fall down. So, in a most ungraceful manner, I collapsed into the nearest pew.

My near faint caused a minimum of excitement. Reverend Nelson paused momentarily, then continued the questioning, and my parents had sense enough not to come running to my aid. Agnes Sjurson, a family friend, did rush out and bring me a glass of water. Her kind attention was mortifying, but the water tasted great and cleared my head. When it came my turn for the last question, I rather shakily stood up. Reverend Nelson was surprised, but quickly recovered and asked my question. I gave the answer and somehow managed to stay on my feet until catechization was over. I was not about to enter the Bergen Congregation sitting on my backside!

Because of the deep, religious feelings of the community and the church-centered social life, Salem and Bergen churches were Roland's two most powerful forces. Nothing was done without first considering whether or not the two churches would approve. There was seldom any trouble since the town's secular leaders were also the moving forces in the churches. This church dominance was not just peculiar to Roland. It was typical of almost all small communities in the midwest.

The church's power was embodied in its pastor. He was the central figure in a community's spiritual, social, and political life. His advice was sought on many diverse questions, and he was often called upon to arbitrate family and business disagreements. If the pastor was a strong willed individual, he could acquire almost baronial control of a town. Many a small town politician found himself in political limbo because of an adverse Sunday morning sermon. Some communities literally became theocracies.

When I was a senior in high school, our community had an unwritten, but very real rule against dancing. Dancing was put in the same sinful category as drinking whiskey and pre-marital sex. Even at our Junior-Senior Proms (known in Roland as banquets) we didn't dance. Instead, we ate, had a short program, then jumped into cars and headed for Des Moines, where we danced and sampled other pleasures of the big city.

Although few of us were wild about dancing, we did feel the rule banning it was silly and archaic, and decided to challenge it. We quietly asked around and, to our surprise, discovered many adults felt as we did. Chaperons were arranged and permission was received to hold the dance in the American Legion Hall. All we had to do was set the date.

None of us had expected such cooperation, and we began to get cold feet. The thought uppermost in our minds was,

"What will the pastors say?" After much discussion, it was decided to inform Reverend Holen, the minister of Salem, and Reverend Nelson of our plans. Those against the idea said we were asking their permission. We, who were for telling them, stoutly maintained that briefing the pastors amounted to nothing more than courtesy calls.

Reverend Olaf Holen greeted the delegation sent to him with a big smile. His smile faded and his natural outgoing friendliness turned cold when he discovered its purpose. In a deep resonant voice that he used with great skill in the pulpit, he let the quaking delegation know that he was opposed to our plan. He went on to state his belief that the dance floor was the devil's playground and didn't want any of his young people from Salem attending the dance. The delegation fled.

Reverend Nelson's response was equally negative; however, he took a calmer, more diplomatic approach. He warned us that our actions would cause problems for ourselves and our parents. That many of the older people were strongly adverse to dancing and that by forcing the issue, the school might lose their support. He wanted us to reconsider whether having a dance was worth the trouble it would cause.

After talking with the pastors, we had another meeting and agreed to scrub the whole idea. We rationalized our decision by saying that none of us really knew how to dance, and that most likely no one would even show up. The naked truth was that dancing wasn't worth facing the wrath of the two ministers.

For someone who has not lived in a small, church-oriented community, it is almost impossible to understand a pastor's unique position. He was, at one and the same time, the town's spiritual counselor, psychiatrist, intellectual, champion of worthy causes, keeper of the public morals and social leader. No man was more respected, loved, and at times, feared. It is little wonder that so many mothers dreamed of having their sons become ministers. To be a minister was to be at the apex of a small community's social structure.

Roland's two pastors were well aware of the multifaceted role of their calling. They also felt keenly the power of their offices. But, to my knowledge, neither ever used his position for self-serving purposes. To their credit, Reverend Nelson and Reverend Holen conducted themselves as shepherds rather than overseers. Both served their God, community, and congregations well.

Bergen and Salem churches still stand and, in appearance, have changed little. The routine of events has changed slightly. Sunday School is now at nine, and the church bells announce the worship services at ten. The spiritual needs of the community are met much as they were when I lived there. Fundamental changes, however, have taken place. The churches no longer are *the* social centers. They still play an important social function, but the role has ceased to be overpowering. The great church suppers are gone, and secular organizations vie equally for the people's time and energy. The parishioner's limited horizons of the 1940s have expanded to include the entire state and beyond. As the horizons of the people broadened, the once awesome power of the churches diminished. No longer does

Sunday morning automatically mean attending church. As in the rest of urban America, golf, swimming, tennis, and boating beckon. Most people of the community are still members of a church and attend regularly. They come to church, not out of fear of social ostracism, but because of deep religious beliefs and the enjoyment of worship. When I return to Roland, I too attend. There is something special about worshipping in my first church home. I feel like I belong, even though half of the congregation does not know who I am. But, that's all right. The walls know. The pews know. And God knows.

✒ Saturday Night In Town

Farmers and their families began arriving as early as five-thirty in the afternoon. My Uncle Sy and Aunt Irene Hall were always among the first. By seven o'clock all of the parking places on Broad Street were taken. An hour later, the cross street Pennsylvania was full, and cars were parked diagonally in the middle of both streets, turning them into boulevards. Sidewalks were crowded. Stores were packed. The movie theatre was full. It was Saturday night in Story City!

If you lived in north Story County, Iowa during the 1940's, Story City was the place to be on Saturday evening. Here the farm wife would shop, socialize, and gossip. The farmer could have a beer, talk about the weather, or gaze longingly at farm machinery he was unable to afford. And the children could see a Roy Rogers, Gene Autry, Randolf Scott, or Lash LeRue epic at the theatre. Saturday night in Story City was a family outing that everyone enjoyed.

For almost all, "going to town" was the social event of the week. However, much to my distress, the Harris Twedt family seldom joined in the fun. There were two major reasons: one, lack of money; two, the hassle of getting five children fed,

Story City Theater.

bathed, and dressed by six-thirty in the evening. As a child, I could understand neither of these sensible and adult reasons. All I knew was that I was missing the excitement.

Since my parents saw fit not to partake of this weekly social feast, I was forced to find other means of getting to Story City. My favorite way was with my cousin, David Twedt. Going with David made the evening even more special. Aunt Mamie and Uncle Leonard went to Story City almost every Saturday night. Mamie's parents had retired to Story, and each Saturday was a mini-family reunion.

On Saturday, I would ride my pony to Uncle Leonard's farm and at sometime in the late afternoon, I'd ask David if he were going to town. He would answer, "Sure. Want to come along?" I, of course, immediately accepted, jumped onto my pony, and rode for home like I was being chased by a sheriff's posse.

"David asked me to go to town with him tonight!" I would yell to Mother as I burst into the kitchen. "Can I go?" Huh? Can I go? Can I, please?"

Usually I went.

If I could not go to Story City with David, I would pester my Uncle Les. This again required me to ride my horse or pony to his farm. Once there, I could not bring myself just to come straight out and beg for a ride. So I would strive to be subtle. The conversation usually went as follows:

ME: (Casually) I hear there's a Lash LeRue movie playing tonight.

LES: (Trying to keep from laughing) You don't say.

ME: Yeah! It's supposed to be really great!

LES: (Dryly) I've heard that Lash LeRue movies are really great.

ME: That's right! Last one I saw old Lash took the guns away from four outlaws with his whip!

LES: Amazing.

ME: Yeah! He's really great!

(Long pause during which I held my breath and turned purple)

LES: You wouldn't want to see this really great movie, would you?

ME: I sure would!

LES: Well, the lawn needs mowing. I'll give you a quarter for cutting it, and you can ride along to town. OK?

There was no question as to what my answer would be. Before he finished speaking, I was running to the shed where he kept his old, reel lawnmower.

Going to Story City with Uncle Les often provided a special treat. Food. Les's wife, Irene, was the daughter of Mr. and Mrs. Sevold, who owned Sevold's Cafe. This cafe was one of the finest in central Iowa. It was especially known for delicious homemade pies. Mrs. Sevold's strawberry-rhubarb pie was a gastronomic miracle. People from twenty and thirty miles away came just to have a piece of pie and some coffee. Sevold's Cafe was one of those small town restaurants that you always look for and almost never find.

Once the arrangements for getting to Story City were completed, the rest of the day was spent in glorious anticipation alternated with fearful concern. The concern was caused by the worry that something unexpected would come up, and I would not be able to go. This happened all too frequently, usually due to machinery breaking down. Instead of going to town, my uncles and Dad would work late into the evening. When this happened, I could be seen walking glumly around the yard stepping on my chin. Disaster that this was to me was generally no big deal to my parents. But, one time, not going turned out to be a *very* big deal.

It was a hot, August Saturday in 1940, and Dad was helping a neighbor, Maynard Johnson, pick sweet corn. The decision to go to the movie had been made the previous night. So, Pete, Herma, and I spent the day with fingers crossed, hoping that Dad would get home on time. Much to our delight, Dad's black 1935 Ford drove up the lane at about four-thirty. Our delight, however, turned to horror when we saw his face. A bumblebee had stung him, and the left-side of his face was so swollen his left eye was shut. One look told us that we were not going to the movies. Dad was in far too much pain. He was in even more pain the following day when he learned that his name had been drawn at the theatre's lottery. The prize was five hundred dollars. And as old timers will remember, five hundred dollars was real money in 1940.

There was a Saturday, six years later, when I wished a bumblebee had stung Uncle Les. He was and is my favorite uncle, but on that day, I would have gladly strangled him.

During the late afternoon, Dad and Uncle Les decided that our old Regular Farmall tractor was needed at Les's farm. The two looked at me, and I immediately protested that I was going to town with David. "No problem," Les informed me. He would have me home in plenty of time. With that, Dad cranked up the Regular, and off I charged. Well, if you call traveling between four and five miles per hour a charge. The Regular had no road gear. It was so slow, I was once passed by four grasshoppers pulling a wagon load of ear corn.

Now, Les had moved that spring, and his new farm was five miles away. This meant I was on the road for over an hour. It was just about the most boring hour of my life. I first sang my repertory of songs, which ranged from the "Maine Hymn" to such classics as "Feudin' A Fussin' and A Fightin'". I then tried counting telephone poles, but it took so long getting from one to the next, I lost count. Finally, I jumped off the tractor and ran along behind it. This actually became quite exciting. I allowed the tractor to drive itself until it almost ran into one of the deep ditches that parallel each side of the road. At the last possible instant, I jumped back onto the tractor and steered onto the middle of the road. This was great fun until I waited a little too long and almost tipped the tractor over.

After what seemed like forever and three weeks, I arrived at Les's farm. My stomach began to churn when I saw his car was not there. I turned off the tractor, ran to the house, and called out to my Aunt Irene. No answer. A quick check of the barn and out buildings revealed that no one was home.

My worst fears were realized. It was after five o'clock, and I had no way to get home. I thought of phoning my folks, but we were on a different exchange than Les. Phoning would have required a long distance call, which in 1946, eleven-year-old boys did not make unless someone was hurt or dying.

What was I to do? I could go into the house an wait for Les to return. But, what if he had forgotten about me? (Which turned out to be what had happened) He might not be home for hours, and Uncle Leonard was picking me up at six-thirty. I ran back into the house. Five-fifteen. Could I run five miles in an hour? Probably not, but I had to try. And, there was the possibility that some kind soul would drive by and give me a ride. I said a silent prayer, cursed my Uncle Les, and tore out of the house.

I had run about two hundred yards when to my right, I saw a swath about twenty feet wide cut through the corn field. The swath, made by some cable company, ran straight as an arrow to our farm. By taking the swath, I would shorten my run by nearly two miles, but doing so would preclude being picked up by a car. I looked up and down the road. Nothing. I then said some words Mother did not know were in my vocabulary, climbed the fence, and began running down the swath.

It was more difficult that I expected. The swath was soft and filled with large clumps, but there was no turning back. I alternately ran and walked, trying not to rest. Due to the tall corn on either side of the swath, there was no breeze. The air was hot, still, and heavy. I was quickly soaked with sweat.

After about a mile, I fell, stumbled to my feet, and fell again. The second time I stayed down. It felt so good just to lie there. But resting on the rich Iowa earth was robbing me of my chance to go to town. I crawled to my feet and forced myself into a slow run.

Because of the heat and the lack of oxygen, I began to hallucinate. Tears mingled with sweat. All I saw was the swath and corn. There was nothing else. The world consisted of rows and rows of corn and this endless swath. I could not remember why I was running, but a voice inside of me kept urging me to continue.

I was close to panic and fainting when I saw a fence, and beyond the fence, a road. When I reached the fence, I leaned against a post and cried. My tears were tears of relief. I have never, before or since, been so happy to see a road.

My head cleared. I looked around and knew where I was. In fact, I could see the top of our barn in the distance. But I was still about a mile from home. There was no way I could make it home in time. One thing was certain. I wanted no more of that swath and corn fields!

I climbed the fence and began trudging my way down the road. After walking less than thirty yards, a car pulled up beside me. It was our neighbor, Rudolph Risdohl. "It looks like you could use a ride, Jerry," he said, in his slow quiet way.

"I sure could," I answered, getting into the car.

Rudy did not say anything until he got the car back up to speed. "Did you fall off a horse?"

"No!" I replied, my anger returning like a sudden summer thunderstorm. "I had to take a tractor over to Uncle Les, and he wasn't home!"

I could see that Rudy did not understand, but I was in no

mood to explain, and he was wise enough not to ask for further clarification. It must have taken a huge amount of self-control not to ask for more details. I, obviously, looked like I had been through a small war. Neither of us said another word until we arrived at the lane to our farm. I thanked Rudy for the ride; he smiled, and drove home. He had a story to tell that night.

I walked up my lane, my anger increasing with every step. By the time I reached the house I was boiling. I slammed the screen door as hard as I could and strode into the kitchen. My family was at the supper table, which made me even more angry. How dare they start eating without me! "Les wasn't there!" I snarled.

My parents were startled. My siblings were shocked. Never had they heard me use that tone of voice when addressing any adult. "What happened to you?" Mother cried.

"I had to run home!" I screamed, glaring accusingly at Dad, as if it were his fault. "Les forgot about me!"

Under normal conditions, such behavior would have earned me a quick trip to the woodshed. But, instead of being angry, Dad looked rather sheepish.

"How'd you get so dirty?" Herma asked.

"I took a shortcut through the field and fell down," I answered, and then turned to Dad. "He promised! Now I can't go to town!"

"Why not?" Pete said. "Leonard hasn't been here yet."

Suddenly, I was the startled one. I glanced at the old Gilbert kitchen clock and saw that it was six-twenty-two. There were still eight minutes before Uncle Leonard would arrive! All was forgotten. I could still go to Story City!

"You wash up," Mother said. "I'll lay out something to wear."

I tore off my clothes, took the fastest sponge bath in recorded history, and ran upstairs. Within minutes, I had changed and was back in the kitchen, where Dad gave me fifty cents while Mother attacked me with a wash cloth. It seems I had missed a place or fourteen. Uncle Leonard drove up the lane, and I bounced out of the door. It is amazing how, when you are eleven, abject dejection can turn swiftly into pure joy.

I mentioned that Dad gave me fifty cents. This was twice the usual amount I received when going to town, and was due to not having time to eat supper. A quarter was enough to provide me with a delightful night. I spent a dime for the movie ticket and a nickel for a bag of popcorn, which left ten cents to be enjoyed after the movie. This dime was spent wisely on a cherry phosphate and a chocolate or strawberry ice cream cone. Now, I ask you, what eleven-year-old could want more than that?

We always approached Story City from the east. My heart began pumping faster when we crossed the Skunk River, which served as the town's eastern boundary. Along the river was the park and the high school football field. In the park, was a foot suspension bridge, which spanned the river and both delighted and frightened most of the small children of north Story County.

After crossing the river, we drove up a slight incline and it was here that the gravel road ended and the red bricks of Broad Street began. There was a moment of triumph when the tires first made contact with the bricks. I had arrived!

Story City's business district was two blocks long, with additional establishments extending one block in either direction on a cross street that separated the two blocks. Buildings were mostly two-story red brick with a few false front wooden structures thrown in. These buildings contained the usual stores required to service a town of two thousand and the area's farmers. Story City was a prosperous, self-contained community. Almost any need, from notions to farm implements, could be purchased. For a time in the late '40s, there were two car dealerships.

But the only business that mattered to the freshly scrubbed children scrambling out of the back seats of Fords, Chevys, Plymouths, and an occasional Buick, was the Story City Theatre. Like me, not one of them could think of a place they would rather be.

The theatre was dominated by a large square marquee painted white with red and blue trim. The top of the marquee had a saw-toothed design. The ends had one large tooth with two smaller ones on each side. The front had two large teeth and four or five smaller ones. A row of white light bulbs accentuated the underside of the marquee. Set back from the street and up a slight incline was the ticket window. On either side of the window were red double doors which led to the promised land.

Once inside, you entered a small lobby. Actually, it was

little more than a wide hallway that ran the width of the fan-shaped theatre. Separating the lobby from the orchestra was a low wall over which hung heavy maroon colored drapes. The drapes could be raised if there were a standing room only crowd. The orchestra, consisting of approximately three-hundred wooden backed, faded upholstered seats, which at one time had been the same color as the drapes, was divided into one large middle section and two smaller wings. It was here that families and younger children enjoyed the movies.

Older children and teenagers gravitated to the balcony's hard wood seats. The balcony was less comfortable, but it was the "groovy" place to sit. There was an unwritten rule, however. The younger teens and those without dates were required to sit in the front. It was understood that the farther one sat back in the balcony, the less interested one was in the movie.

I was always interested in the movie. I could not understand anyone who was not, which shows you how young and innocent I was. There have been few film goers less discriminating than myself. If the pictures moved and words were spoken, I was enthralled. Had I lived in a city, I would have been one of those kids who sat through a movie two or three times.

Only once in my formative years did a movie fail to capture me. That was the night of the great Story City Theatre soybean war.

The first skirmish of the war occurred on the Saturday night before the main battle. A few boys had brought bean shooters and delighted in "beaning" the other kids. All the other boys swore that they would be armed and ready for the next Saturday night movie.

Perhaps, for the uninitiated, I should explain how a bean shooter works. Think of it as a mini blowgun. All that is required is a round tube just slightly larger than a soybean, the bean itself, and lung power. A good shooter could fire a bean fifteen to twenty feet.

On the night of the war, David and I claimed our usual seats in the front row of the balcony. We quickly learned this was a mistake and the wisdom of the old military adage, "take the high ground". The first row was a great place to see a movie, but a lousy place from which to fight a war.

The opening credits of Lash LeRue lit up the screen at the same moment a hail storm of soybeans struck the balcony. David and I were both hit in the first volley, causing us to dive beneath our seats for protection. The flying beans were as thick as flack over Berlin in World War II! Within seconds, the cries of pain, shouts of triumph, and the ratta-tata-tat of soybeans drowned out the movie sound track. The war was on!

David and I were in a dilemma. If we stayed beneath the seats, we were safe; however, being safe meant we could not shoot anyone else. The desire to fight won out. We popped up, blew for all we were worth, then dove back under the seats to reload. This worked quite well until I was struck in the forehead, which in turn caused me to swallow the bean I was about to shoot! The bean went down the wrong pipe, and I spent the next few seconds afraid I was going to choke. Luckily, I coughed it up. Did I learn anything from this close call? Don't be silly! As soon as I could breathe normally, I was back firing.

By now the balcony was in chaos. Kids were dashing up and down the aisles, falling over seats, shouting, crying, and generally having a wonderful time. At this point, the owner ran up the stairs, yelling for us to stop. For a moment there was a pause. Then, as if pre-planned, every bean shooter zeroed in on him. The poor man must have felt like a missionary being attacked by Pygmies. He fled down the stairs, cursing his fate, our parents, and us. We cheered, then returned to the joyous task of shooting each other.

The furor mounted until kids in the orchestra were standing on their seats looking back up at the balcony. The movie was forgotten. The show in back was much better than the one on the screen. But, all good things must come to an end.

Suddenly, a powerful flashlight beam pierced the darkness and caught us like scurrying cockroaches. The beam was accompanied with a loud male voice. "You kids sit down and shut up!" It was one of the town's two policemen. Never has a police officer looked so huge! The balcony became as quiet as an empty library. "Sit down in your seats or I'll throw you all out of here and tell your parents!"

No order was ever obeyed so swiftly. Like mice dashing for their holes, we ran to our seats. "And if I have to come back up here, some of you just might learn what the inside of a real jail looks like!" Now, this was the '40s, not the '60s. There was no thought of confronting an angry police officer. The war was over. We sat as still as porcelain figures. I doubt if any audience ever watched a Lash LeRue movie with such concentration.

While the children were cheering on the likes of Lash LeRue, the adults enjoyed good conversation. It was almost impossible to walk ten feet without meeting someone you knew. Between shopping and visiting, two hours were required to journey up one side of Broad Street and down the other. Stops at the Five and Ten Cent Store, Alsagers Meat Market, and the Pioneer Store were mandatory. If the males of the family needed clothes, time was spent below the slowly revolving ceiling fans of Charleson's Clothing Store or Starky and Kenutson Men's Wear. And, if there was a little extra cash, a cup of coffee and a piece of pie at Sevold's Cafe was a special treat. Also, at the cafe, you were sure to talk with people you had missed on the street. By evening's end, any news of importance was shared and most secrets, told in strictest confidence, were common knowledge.

Between nine and nine-thirty, the theatre disgorged north Story County's future farmers and homemakers, or so everyone thought at the time. Little did we know how few would stay in the state of Iowa. Younger children ran directly to their family's car. Older ones broke into groups of three and four and joined the Broad Street promenade. Teenagers segregated themselves by sex and also broke into small groups. The girls dashed across the street, so as to walk the business district clockwise. This way they could accidentally run into the boys who were making the same circuit counter clockwise. And, by some strange coincidence, this meeting often took place in front of Jacobson's Drug Store. If a girl played her cards right, she stood a good chance of sharing an ice cream soda or a malted milk shake with the boy of her choice. Younger girls would see this and try the same tactic on some boy whose hormones had yet to be awakened. Instant rebuff! Why should any boy want to share such a delicacy with a dumb girl? Several years and biological changes would answer the question.

Ten o'clock was the witching hour. Stores closed, sleepy children were piled into back seats, and, within minutes, the red brick streets of Broad and Pennsylvania were nearly empty.

If I had gone to town with David, we would wave our good-byes to friends and walk a few blocks east and south to his grandparents' house. I remember these walks as being very pleasant. There was certainly no thought of danger. Almost every house had people sitting on the front porch, who paused in their conversations to note our passing. They might have not known our names, but they knew to which families we belonged. We couldn't have been safer asleep in our own beds.

Part of the enjoyment of that walk was listening to the radio. No, we didn't have portables. We did not need them. Nearly every home had its radio turned on and tuned to WHO's Iowa Barn Dance Frolic. We could walk down the street and not miss a note of a song by "The Song Fellows," or the punch line of a Cliff Carl joke. We in no way thought this was exceptional. It was just the way things were in small town America during the 1940's.

Grandpa and Grandma Jacobson lived in a white, two-story

frame house. We entered through an enclosed front porch, which led into the dining room. Nine chances out of ten, we found Grandma Jacobson, her daughters, and daughters-in-law busily setting out small plates and coffee cups for a snack. To the left of the dining room was a small parlor where the men of the family sat smoking and discussing crops, hog prices, and the weather. The room was a non-smoker's nightmare. Every male was puffing away on a cigar, pipe, or cigarette. It must have taken Grandma Jacobson a week to air out the place.

Once David and I had checked in and perhaps mooched a cookie, we went out into the back yard and played tag or hide-n-seek with our cousins. I say "our" because most were my cousins, as well as his. The Twedt and Jacobson clans had a definite attraction for each other. Leonard Twedt married Mamie Jacobson. Gaylord Jacobson, Mamie's brother, married Jurina Twedt, Leonard's sister. And to add to the confusion, Mamie's brother, Millard Jacobson, married Olive Branjord, who was my mother's sister. Because of this interchange of marital vows, I was considered one of the brood.

Being treated as one of Grandma Jacobson's grandchildren was more important to me than she ever knew. I had no grand-mother. My grandmother Twedt died three months before I was born. And my grandmother Branjord died when I was seven. So, whenever I went to town with David, I pretended that Grandma Jacobson was my grandmother, too. She was a sweet, kindly woman with knowing eyes which had seen most of the good and bad life had to offer. I don't remember her ever holding me or giving me a kiss, but she smiled at me, and that was enough.

Grandma Jacobson was also an excellent baker. Her spice cake topped with real whipped cream still makes my mouth water. We would all sit down at the dining room table and have a piece before leaving for our individual homes. The evening was not complete unless it ended with a piece of spice cake. The cake was delicious, but there is no doubt that it was extra special because it was made by Grandma Jacobson.

Once the cake was eaten, the coffee drunk, and the good-byes said for the third or fourth time, David and I crawled into the back seat of Leonard's blue 1940 two-door Ford, and we started for home. Generally, both of us were asleep before we left the brick streets of Story City. Mamie awoke me when we reached our farm. I sleepily pushed my way out of the car, thanked Leonard and Mamie for taking me, then contentedly went to bed. Saturday night in Story City was over.

Sadly, by 1955, Saturday night in Story City was permanently over. Stores were closed by six o'clock. Choice parking places on Broad Street went begging. The theatre was open, but those attending came specifically to see the show. No one was in town for the fun of being there. Saturday night was as quiet as any Tuesday. Farmers, like everyone else, were watching "Your Show of Shows," and professional wrestling from Chicago. An institution was destroyed by a fuzzy black and white picture beamed almost magically into every house. Mass communication replaced one-on-one conversation. A window to the world was opened. A door to the community was closed. I will not argue that the gain was not worth the cost. But something very warm, something very human, was lost. I am thankful I was able to have experienced it.

An interesting postscript: By some miracle, the Story City Theatre, that I so dearly love, did not close. Somehow, it hung on, and in the 1980's was declared an historic landmark. It looks almost the same now as it did in the 1940's. So, if you are traveling I-35 between Des Moines and Minneapolis and have some time, stop by and take in a show. If you, however, choose to sit in the balcony, be careful where you walk. There still might be some soybeans around.

◆ **The Factory**

Silence, where there should be noise, screams at you like a child's empty room after the child has died. This is the silence that surrounds the Marshall Canning Company. The crumbling, backward "L" shaped, two-story, red brick building slowly rots like a decaying corpse on the northeastern edge of Roland. It looks at the town with shattered, dead eyes. What was once a source of pride is now something to be ignored. Only the town's "gray beards" remember when its belt-driven machinery rattled and clanked fifteen to eighteen hours a day from early June to mid-September.

The Marshall Canning Company, known to all local inhabitants as "the factory," was constructed in 1918. Sweet corn and peas were canned at the factory until 1944. Then, because World War II made it more profitable for farmers to raise other crops, the peas were discontinued. Canning corn continued until 1958.

The factory provided fewer than ten men with full time employment, yet it was of great importance to the town and the surrounding community. It provided Roland with a tax base,

Marshall Canning Company, early '40s.

gave farmers a cash crop, allowed housewives to build a little nest egg of their own, and served as an introduction to the working world for teenagers. In one way or another, most of the people who lived within a six mile radius of the town gained some direct or indirect benefit from the factory.

I first became aware of its existence when I was five. The year was 1940. Dad had picked a wagon load of sweet corn and asked Pete, Herma, and myself if we wanted to ride to town with him. We were in the wagon before he finished the question.

Max and Lady, a team of draft horses who were as gray in spirit as they were in color, pulled the wagon to Roland while Pete, Herma, and I happily stripped the husks off ears of delicious corn. We approached the town from the north. Just before reaching the Minneapolis and St. Louis railroad tracks, we turned east for two blocks, and there, smoke pouring from its tall chimney, was the factory. It was a block away, but the size of the building made me crawl close to my father.

Now, you have to understand that as factories go, the Marshall Canning Company was relatively small. But to a five-year-old who had never seen anything larger than Bergen Lutheran Church, it was awesome and more than a little frightening. Adding to my alarm were the unfamiliar factory sounds which, like the angry growls of some pre-historic monsters, emanated from the colossus. My father did not even own a tractor, so the noise made by machinery was completely foreign.

Dad pulled the horses to a stop where the paved street ended and the dirt lane began, and muttered something under his breath that I am sure my mother was happy I did not catch. He was upset because there were about fifteen wagons waiting to unload. He became even more upset when, with each passing minute, my brother, my sister, and I grew increasingly bored. Finally, he could take the whining trio no longer and allowed us to climb down from the wagon and walk to a grassy commons which was just south of the factory office. We were given strict orders to not go near the factory.

Sooo... well, what would you have done if you were five? The incredible noise coming through the open windows was like a siren call. As I played tag with my siblings, I kept glancing at the steps which I later learned led to the husking room. My chance to investigate came when two other children arrived on the commons. Pete and Herma began playing with them and failed to notice that I was easing my way toward the factory. I checked to see if Dad were watching, then walked across the gravel path that separated the commons from the factory. I was, as we used to say, scared stiff. But I was more curious than scared. I climbed the four wooden steps and peeked inside.

What my wide eyes saw was a dim, large room with a rough heavy planked floor. Squatting on that floor, like giant hungry dragons, were the green husking machines. Feeding those machines were men whose arms were a blur of motion. I thought for sure their fingers would be caught in the rollers which ripped the husk from the corn. The noise was deafening. I took a tentative step inside. The green dragons seemed to call me, "Closer...come closer". I was almost next to the first machine when its operator noticed me. He look startled. Then it was my turn to be startled. Two familiar large hands scooped me up and carried me out of the factory. "What did I tell you?" Dad said, as he gave me a swat on the fanny and carried me back to the wagon. I did not answer. I stared at the factory and wondered if one day I would work there and feed those angry dragons. The answer turned out be yes and no. Yes, I worked at the factory. No, I never fed the husking machines.

My first job at the factory came when I was sixteen. I was hired as a clean up boy in the canning room. Did the factory need a clean up boy? Probably not. But the general manager, George Thornblade, knew I needed a job, so he created one. This was the way things were down at the factory and, undoubtedly, was one of the reasons it went out of business.

Allow me, at this point, to give you a thirty-five cent tour of the factory by following an ear of corn through the canning process. The corn was unloaded into a hopper and elevated to a raked wooden holding floor. From here it was conveyed to a two-story wood frame building, which had been added to the brick structure. The first floor of this building housed my friends the green dragons. Once the corn was fed through the husking machines, it was elevated to the second floor, where it was dumped unto a long white slow moving conveyer belt. The belt was about forty-eight inches wide. Women sat on either side of the belt an culled out the nubbins and faulty corn. If part of an ear was bad, the damaged part was cut away and the rest of the ear sent through the system. The corn dropped from the white belt onto a conveyer that elevated it into the main building and onto another long white belt, which ran the length of the cutting room. Here, more women fed the ears into cutting machines. The cobs were stripped naked and sent to the waste pile, while the golden kernels were augured down to the first floor canning room. The corn was then divided between two machines: one filled gallon cans, the other sixteen ounce cans. Once the cans were sealed, they were stacked in heavy steel baskets, which were lowered into large cylindrical cookers. Each cooker could hold three or four baskets. I know little of the cookers because they were off limits to everyone but the man who operated them. This area of the factory was considered especially dangerous, and unless you had a reason to be there, the management demanded you stay clear. After the corn had been cooked, the baskets were hoisted out of the cookers and hooked onto a slow moving track, which emersed the baskets in a long narrow cooling trough. Almost an hour was needed for each basket to wade its way through the trough. After the basket had completed playing submarine, the track delivered it into the warehouse, where the cans were removed and placed into boxes. The corn was now ready for labeling. And what labels were put on the cans? Answer: whatever company bought the product. One day, Monarch labels were slapped onto the cans. The next day, Green Giant. The third, Jack Sprat. Same corn, different labels. All who worked at the factory smiled when they heard some woman extolling the quality of one brand over another. And, as for me, seeing the different labels being put on the cans has given me a life long suspicion of "brand names".

As I mentioned earlier, my first job was that of clean up boy in the canning room. This large damp area was dominated by the two canning lines. The process, even back then, was mostly automated. One man ran the gallon line, and two patrolled the sixteen ounce line. Empty cans were fed by gravity from the second floor on metal racks that were fastened to the walls. The cans ended up on a conveyer which marched them like little tin soldiers beneath a filling nozzle. A pre-set amount of corn and brine was dumped into each can. Lids were then secured by another machine and the cans were ready for the cookers. The system ran remarkably trouble free. One reoccurring problem, however, was empty cans getting hung up on the racks. The machine operator had to keep a careful watch, or there would be corn all over the floor.

The worst spill I remember was caused by the novel, "I, The Jury". The young man running the sixteen-ounce line was at the climax of the book--the part where the girl takes off her clothes and walks toward Mike Hammer--and he was oblivious to everything but the written page and his scorching imagination. I was the first to see the huge pile of corn on the floor. I began yelling, but due to the noise and the fact his mind was buried between the woman's perfectly formed cup shaped breasts, he did not hear me. My voice was soon joined by the other operator and that of the foreman's. No response. The proverbial bomb could have gone off and the young man would not have noticed. The foreman ran to the machine and shut down the line. Only then did the glassy eyed reader come back to the mundane world of canning corn. The foreman ripped up the book and told the amazed culprit that he would be fired if he were ever again caught reading a book while the line was running. I don't know if the poor guy ever did learn how the book ended. I do know my back hurt after shoveling all that corn down the drain.

Come to think of it, breasts almost got me fired about a week later. The lines were running well, which left me with little to do. So, I decided to do some exploring. My first stop was the brine mixing room, where huge vats of brine were being prepared. The vats reminded me of huge fairy tale mixing bowls illustrated in *Jack and the Beanstalk*. However, interesting as it was to see the brine man mix the contents with a canoe paddle, the smell soon drove me from the room.

I wandered back to the warehouse, where I helped the cooker push some baskets into the cooling trough. After receiving a rather surprised "thank you", I started back to where the casing crew was putting cans into boxes. I hadn't gone ten steps when I noticed two women and a teenage girl sitting on low stools, pounding dents out of empty cans. Rounding out the cans was necessary because dented cans were prone to hanging up in the canning racks. I knew the girl and went over to say hello. I had no intention of staying for any length of time, but as I approached the girl, I noticed that she was wearing an off-the-shoulder peasant blouse. I further noticed that, when she bent over to pound on the can, much of what the blouse was meant to cover became visible. Any thought of continuing on to the casing crew vanished from my suddenly feverish, little mind. I attempted to be cool and make conver -

sation while my eyes minutely surveyed the girl's well endowed chest. I know I failed because the two older women could not completely smother their laughter as I babbled on, and the young lady found it more and more necessary to bend over. The fun ended when my foreman sneaked up behind me and informed everyone within half a mile that I was paid to clean up, not to look down the blouses of young women! I blushed and fled. But, as the days passed, I saw that the young lady often wore the peasant blouse. This caused me a dilemma; should I stay with my push broom in the canning room or risk losing my job by finding excuses to go back into the girl's work area? It was a classic choice--money or cleavage. I pondered the decision for nearly five seconds. The right side of my brain said stay, but the left side had already put my feet into motion. Hey! I was sixteen years old. Besides, Dad had stressed to me that money isn't everything.

Anyone who worked at the factory had to be somewhat philosophical about money. Even for the '50s the pay was low. Men received ninety cents per hour an women eighty cents. But, since the work was seasonal, and there were rumors of the factory closing down, nobody complained too loudly. I was, however, puzzled by the ten cents discrepancy between men and women. Why was I, a clean up boy, making ninety cents when a woman running a machine was paid eighty cents? I asked the foreman, who shrugged and answered, "That's just the way it is".

"But that doesn't seem fair," I replied.

The foreman glared at me. "Do you want to be paid eighty cents?"

"No, sir."

"Then stop asking stupid questions!"

I stopped. However, the question was not stupid. I cannot say as much for the answer.

My most enjoyable working experience at the factory came the following summer. I was assigned to care for six machines in the cutting room. I greased the machines in the morning and cleaned them when the work day was over. In between, six women fed them the sweetest corn on the planet. The kernels were stripped from the cob by small razor sharp blades attached to a spinning plate with a hole in the center. Springs attached to the blades and plate allowed the blades to adjust to the different size ears of corn. Frequently, cobs became jammed in the blades, at which time it became my job to free up the machine without breaking the blades and, more important to me, not cutting my fingers. After a few broken blades and the loss of a little blood, I became quite proficient.

When the machines were running well, I spent a goodly amount of time giving the women back rubs. Not only the women who ran my six machines, but most of the women on the front side of the room. Sixteen hours or more of feeding the cutting machines were killing on the neck and shoulder muscles. Although I now realize that the older women were most in need of the massage, it was the younger ones who received the lion's share of attention. And it will come as no surprise that the prettier they were, the longer and more dedicated was the rub. The sighs, moans, and "Oh, that feels so good," was pretty exciting stuff for an innocent farm boy. Especially when they leaned back against me. I was too dumb to realize that some of those women might have enjoyed having other parts of their anatomies massaged.

One sweet young thing, only a few years older than myself, attempted to prod me into action by introducing me to pornography. One day, she handed me a green theme folder and with a wicked glint in her eyes said, "Read this!"

The folder's color was appropriate, for the title that greeted my seventeen-year-old eyes was, *Behind the Green Door*. I began reading there by the machines, but by page two had fled to a rather dark stairwell. Doubtlessly, this disappointed the young woman, who, I'm sure, wanted to see my "reaction".

And react I did! It took me about twenty minutes to read the story, and nearly an equal amount of time before I could leave the stairwell without being embarrassed. Was I shocked? Absolutely. I had no idea such material existed. And, more to the point, I was dumfounded that people did those things. Could it be that such goings on occurred in Roland, Iowa? Impossible! Yet, my sex life consisted of nothing but fantasies. How was I to know? It was a highly excited and confused young man who came out of the stairwell and tried to casually walk back to the cutting machines.

"What'd you think?" The young woman smirked.

"Whew!" was my reply, as I handed the folder back to her. She laughed and slipped the sizzling pages into her tote bag.

For the next few days, she looked at me rather quizzically,

then, when she saw I was not about to rise to the occasion, she became cold and began to ignore me. I was surprised and hurt by this reaction. Try as I might, I could not figure out what I had done to deserve such treatment. I had much to learn.

When the machines were finally shut down for the day, the men stayed an extra hour to clean up. First, high pressure water hoses were used to clean the machines and floor. Then, heavy, two inch hoses were unrolled, and the machines were bathed in live steam. Manning the steam hoses required strength and care. Nobody messed around with the steam hoses. Not so the water hoses. Putting high pressure water hoses into the hands of teenage boys was inviting world class water fights!

The fights inevitably began after we were finished steaming the equipment. The entire room was deep in fog. Often, it was impossible to see more than five feet in any direction. Then, out of nowhere would come a soaking stream of water, and the water fight was on!

The best part of the fight was feeling your way around the machines, trying to sneak up on the other guy, who was attempting to do the same to you. Even though I served in the peacetime army, these water fights were as close to real combat as I got. My eyes strained to see through the fog. Every nerve ending seemed to vibrate. Any sound stopped me dead in my tracks. I hardly dared breathe. Many times, as in real combat, we passed within yards of each other and didn't even know it.

The water fight that I remembered most vividly (naturally,

I won) began when I had just finished steaming the last of my six machines. I was hanging up the hose when the stream of water splattered on the window next to me. I ran for my water hose and the stalking began. The fog was still thick, but I knew it would clear in a few minutes. I decided to set a trap. I climbed up on one of the machines, laid flat on the large white conveyer belt, and waited. I was no sooner in position when an almost invisible figure crept below me through the fog. I allowed him to pass, then opened the nozzle. Bull's eye! He swung around to hit me, but had no idea where I was. I held the water on him until he dropped his hose and fled for the door. I yelled triumphantly as my stream of water followed him. But the cry was short lived. Just as my friend reached the open doorway, the night watchman walked through it. Drenchville! The man was closer to seventy than seventeen and was not amused. I was sure I would be fired. But a thorough ass chewing was my only punishment. I learned my lesson, however. I did not get into another water fight for...well, at least twenty-four hours.

The cleanup was usually over around one or two in the morning. I would then walk to my brother, Pete's, home for four or five hours of sleep. He and his new bride, Viola Mae, lived about four or five blocks directly south of the factory. I remember those walks with great fondness. The town was as quiet as any deep woods campsite. My way was lit by an occasional street light, moonbeams filtered through stately elms and sprawling oaks, and some late partying fireflies. The soft summer night enveloped me with a wonderful sense of security.

There was no meanness on these streets. Nothing to fear. Nothing to dread. Instead, there was a deep peace and a deeper sense of belonging. My world in 1952 was a gentle one.

Forty years later my world is hectic, filled with the noise and activity of modern urban living. By contrast, the Marshall Canning Company is as still as the quiet streets I once walked. The factory's last corn pack was in 1958. The building stood empty for a few years, before a small furniture company rented the facility. This enterprise limped along for a number of years, then it, too, failed. There is currently talk of another concern buying the factory, but that's all it is...talk. Chances are the building will continue to rot until it collapses or is bulldozed. When the end does come, it will cause a twinge of pain for those of us who remember when lights burned into the early hours of the morning and belt driven machinery enthralled and frightened little boys. Sleep well, my dragons, sleep well.

Epilogue

The past forty years have brought profound changes to the Roland community. The lifestyle of my boyhood has gone the way of Scarlet O'Hara's antebellum South. The family farm described in the preceding pages is as extinct as Tara. Roland has grown in population, yet the school has been torn down, there is only one grocery store, and no hardware stores. The town no longer depends on agriculture for its existence. Instead, it has become a bedroom community for Ames. Roland is mostly composed of elderly and commuters. However, one thing has not changed. The land. The rich earth is still planted in the spring, cultivated in the summer, and gives up of its abundance in the fall. For those of us who left the farm, the land serves as a link to our pasts.

The young boy who out stubborned Tony, drove horses on the threshing run, and walked the wooden floors of Roland Consolidated School, has journeyed through young adulthood, passed through middle-age, and is rapidly approaching retirement. My life has been urban, not rural. The amenities my childhood lacked—indoor plumbing, hot running water, central heating, and air conditioning -- long ago became necessities. I accept them now as I once accepted a cook range in the kitchen and a water pail on the sink.

Thinking back on the decade of the '40s from the warmth of my Florida patio, I sometimes wonder if I am the same person who stood shivering in front of a space heater before going out into the cold early morning darkness to milk cows. My adult life has been so far removed from the events of this book that they seem almost to have happened to someone else. Light years of difference separate the boy who rode horses and the man who produced and directed television shows.

Yet, for years I was able to build a bridge between man and boy. By standing in a hot shower and putting a steamy washcloth over my face, I could feel exactly like I did when I stood in front of the space heater on a frigid Iowa morning. For a few precious seconds, a time warp was created. Man and boy were united. I could once again experience the years when dreams were vivid and all things were possible. But, of late, I no longer can reach the boy. I come tantalizingly close, but the gulf of years has become too great. I have resigned myself to the fact he is forever lost in the mists of time past. I miss him. I miss him very much.

I·O·W·A
HERITAGE
COLLECTION

An ever-expanding series of original books and classic reprints about Iowa, selected for insightful portrayals of the state and its people.

As Ding Saw Herbert Hoover by Jay N. Darling
The Attic: A Memoir by Curtis Harnack
Buggies, Blizzards, and Babies by Cora Frear Hawkins
A Change and a Parting: My Story of Amana by Barbara S. Yambura with Eunice Willis Bodine
Crinoline to Calico by Nan Heacock
Ding: The Life of Jay Norwood Darling by David L. Lendt
Esther's Town by Deemer Lee
Exploring Buried Buxton: Archaeology of an Abandoned Iowa Coal Mining Town with a Large Black Population by Davis M. Gradwohl and Nancy M. Osborn
Frontierswomen: The Iowa Experience by Glenda Riley
Grant Wood and Marvin Cone: Artists of an Era by Hazel Brown
Growing Up in Iowa edited by Clarence A. Andrews
Growing Up in the 40s: Rural Reminiscence by Jerry L. Twedt
A History of Iowa by Leland L. Sage
In No Time at All by Carl Hamilton
Iowa Inside Out by Herb Hake
It's Hard to Look Graceful When You're Dragging Your Feet by Helen Foster
Journey to Autonomy: A Memoir by Louise Rosenfield Noun
A Judge and a Rope and Other Stories of Bygone Iowa by George Mills
The Little Man with the Long Shadow: The Life and Times of Frederick M. Hubbell by George S. Mills
Looking in Windows: Surprising Stories of Old Des Moines by George Mills
Memories of an Iowa Farm Boy by H. E. Wilkinson
Old Orchard Farm by Hugh Orchard
Out of This World: Poems from the Hawkeye State by Gary Gildner and Judith Gildner
A Peculiar People: Iowa's Old Order Amish by Elmer Schwieder and Dorothy Schwieder
Prairie City, Iowa: Three Seasons at Home by Douglas Bauer
Pure Nostalgia: Memories of Early Iowa by Carl Hamilton
The Rise and Fall of the Mustache and Other "Hawk-Eyetems" by Robert J. Burdette
Rogues and Heroes from Iowa's Amazing Past by George Mills
Stories from under the Sky by John Madson
Strong-Minded Women: The Emergence of the Woman-Suffrage Movement in Iowa by Louise R. Noun
Tales Out of School by Verl Crow Shoemaker
Tarpleywick: A Century of Iowa Farming by Henry C. Taylor
Threads of Memory: A Memoir of the 1920s by Margaret Ott Onerheim
We Have All Gone Away by Curtis Harnack
When We Went First Class: A Recollection of Good Times by Ellen Williamson
The Worlds between Two Rivers: Perspectives on American Indians in Iowa edited by Gretchen M. Bataille, David M. Gradwohl, and Charles P. Silet